INTO
SPACE

BOOKS BY ARTHUR C. CLARKE

Nonfiction
THE CHALLENGE OF THE SPACESHIP
PROFILES OF THE FUTURE
VOICES FROM THE SKY
THE PROMISE OF SPACE

Fiction
ISLANDS IN THE SKY
CHILDHOOD'S END
THE CITY AND THE STARS
2001: A SPACE ODYSSEY

And Others

BOOKS BY ROBERT SILVERBERG

Nonfiction
LOST CITIES AND VANISHED CIVILIZATIONS
SCIENTISTS AND SCOUNDRELS
THE MORNING OF MANKIND
THE WORLD OF SPACE

Fiction
TIME OF THE GREAT FREEZE
THE GATE OF WORLDS
NIGHTWINGS
TOWER OF GLASS

And Others

INTO
SPACE

a young person's guide to space

by
ARTHUR C. CLARKE
and
ROBERT SILVERBERG

Revised Edition

HARPER & ROW, PUBLISHERS
New York, Evanston, San Francisco, London

Contents

Preface

Early in 1953, I wrote a book for young people called *Going Into Space;* the British edition was entitled *The Young Traveller In Space.* At that time, the largest rocket in existence was the 14-ton V-2 missile, and the greatest distance any object had ever travelled from Earth was 250 miles.

Rather a lot has happened, therefore, since *Going Into Space* was written: in fact, about half the "future developments" I described then have already occurred. Despite this, the book continued to sell steadily; and the more out-of-date it grew, the more embarrassed I became. However, I have been far too busy with Space Odysseys, hauling up sunken treasure from the Indian Ocean, watching Apollo launches, playing with dolphins, and other humdrum matters to do anything about it.

I am therefore delighted that my friend Robert Silverberg—who is also one of the best science fiction writers in the business—has completely revised the text and brought it up to date. As it is now virtually a new book, I have changed the title to *Into Space.*

The other day, when I was visiting NASA, one of the younger astronauts produced a copy of my first book; he had won it as a prize while a boy at school. I would like to think that *this* book may have been the inspiration for some future space explorer fifteen or twenty years from now on his way to Mars.

Arthur C. Clarke
Colombo, Ceylon

List of Plates

(Plates will be found in a group following page 50)

xii   ●   LIST OF PLATES

List of Figures

xiii

1

Voyages in Space

Man is the great explorer. Perhaps a million years ago, our remote ancestors began to spread over the face of the world until at last they had made their homes in every continent except the frozen Antarctic. The final chapter in the long story of Earth's exploration was not written until our own age. Now, thanks to the conquest of the air, no spot on the globe is more than a few hours' distance from any other, and our astronauts have circled the world in ninety minutes.

It is hard for us to remember that, only sixty or seventy years ago, there were great areas of the Earth where no man had ever been. Our grandfathers could dream, when they read such adventure stories as *King Solomon's Mines*, of strange countries and peoples still waiting to be discovered. Now that the airplane has helped to fill in the last blanks on the map, the mystery and romance which always surround the unknown have been swept away. The world is a more humdrum and a less exciting place.

Or so it seems at first sight. The truth of the matter is that, although we may have explored the continents, we have scarcely scratched the surface even of our own planet. The ocean deeps—three-quarters of the Earth—are still as unknown as was Darkest Africa in the middle of the nineteenth century. And in the other direction, above the atmosphere, lies the enormous emptiness of space. Shining out there in the darkness we can see other worlds than ours—the Moon, the planets, and the still more distant stars. The first explorers from Earth have already walked the face of the Moon; our adventure into the newest and most vast of all frontiers is only beginning, however, and the years to come will see a series of stunning achievements in discovery, rivaling and surpassing those of centuries gone by. We have started to fulfill one of mankind's oldest and most fantastic dreams: we are escaping from our native planet to go voyaging out into space, to other worlds.

Before we examine man's present and future accomplishments in the realm of space, let us look for a moment into the past to find out how the idea of interplanetary flight first arose. In ancient times, before the invention of the telescope, no one knew that there *were* any worlds other than our own. With the unaided eye one could see that great fireball the Sun, of course. One could see the stars by night—but, looking at them, one would never be able to guess that those twinkling points of light were blazing suns, most of them millions of times larger than the world on which we live. Such an idea seems against all common sense, so it is not surprising that it was a long time before anyone could prove it was true, and longer still before everybody else believed it.

Most of the stars seemed to stand still—each in its proper place, fixed and unmoving, a glowing point in the pattern of the constellations. But a few "stars" had no fixed place, and seemed to travel freely in the heavens; men called them the "wanderers." (In Greek, the word for "wanderer" was *planetes,* from which our word "planet" comes.) Without telescopes, though, no one could know that these wandering "stars" were worlds.

Even the Moon, our nearest neighbor, was too far away for the naked eye to tell us much about it, though some of the Greek scientists more than 2,000 years ago had been able to make a good estimate of its size. They knew it must be a world in its own right, and not just a small globe only a few miles away; but what kind of world it was, they could not tell.

The invention of the telescope late in the 16th century changed all this. In 1609, the Italian scientist Galileo looked through his crude, homemade telescopes and discovered new lands in the sky. Although the best instrument Galileo used was not as good as a pair of modern field glasses, he could see the mountains and plains on the Moon and was even able to map its surface. After that date, men knew definitely that the Earth was not the only world that existed, and they also began to wonder if we were the only people in the universe. To *that* question, we still do not know the answer—but one day we will.

It is not surprising that the discoveries of Galileo and later astronomers excited enormous interest. Men began to ask themselves what it was like in the new lands they could dimly see through their feeble telescopes. They tried to imagine the kinds of creatures that might live there. And, before long, they started wondering if explorers would ever be able to cross space as they had already crossed the sea.

This, remember, was three hundred years ago. We think

of space flight as a modern idea, and so it is rather startling to learn that several stories of voyages to the Moon (and the Sun!) were written by the French poet Cyrano de Bergerac as long ago as 1656. Plate 1, taken from Cyrano's *Voyages to the Moon and Sun,* shows what may well be considered as the first of all imaginary spaceships. Like many other spaceships in fiction since that day, alas, it wouldn't have worked. The idea was that magnifying glasses would concentrate the sun's rays into the sphere in which Cyrano is sitting, and that the heated air would then rush out and drive the vehicle upward by a form of jet-propulsion! All that would have happened in practice, of course, is that Cyrano would soon have been cooked by the concentrated sunlight, but the sphere wouldn't have budged. And today we know that there is no air between us and the Moon, so such an arrangement couldn't possibly have worked once it left the atmosphere.

During the next two hundred years, many other writers produced tales of journeys to the Moon, but few of them were intended at all seriously. At the same time, astronomical knowledge steadily increased. A good deal was discovered about the Earth's atmosphere—that invisible blanket which enables us to breathe and which protects us from space—and the forces which make the planets move were better understood.

The first man to use all this new knowledge was the famous French writer Jules Verne, who foresaw so many of our modern inventions, such as the submarine and the helicopter. His novel *From the Earth to the Moon,* which was published in 1865, contained a remarkable amount of accurate scientific information, and is still well worth reading today (much of it is also highly amusing). Verne knew that nothing depending on the air could possibly fly to the Moon, which ruled out balloons and machines using wings or propellers. But if one could build an enormous gun, and fire a shell from it in the right direction *and* with enough speed, it would be possible to hit the Moon. It is not hard to calculate what starting speed the shell would need, nor how long the journey would take, and Verne was very careful to get all his figures right. Where he let his imagination go, however, was in pretending that men traveling in such a shell would not be killed by the concussion when the gun was fired, no matter how well padded and protected they might be (Plate 2).

However, even if we now know there were flaws in Verne's ideas, they were brilliantly worked out, and they must have made many people think seriously about travel through space. The shell inside which his voyagers circled the Moon was fitted with apparatus to supply oxygen, observation windows through which the travelers could watch the stars, and—the most modern touch of all—rockets for steering. More than a hundred years ago, Verne realized that rockets could be used to give a "push" in the vacuum of space and so would be invaluable in guiding a spaceship.

Since Jules Verne's time, there have been thousands of stories about space flight. One of the finest, at least from the literary point of view, is H.G. Wells' *The First Men in the Moon*, written in 1901, two years before the first airplane left the ground. It conveys beautifully the wonder and mystery of other worlds, and no reader will ever forget Wells' description of the lunar dawn, or his hero's adventures in the buried empire of the "Selenites." It is true that the Moon, as we know today, is somewhat different from the place Wells imagined. Yet I think that men will still be reading his book with enjoyment long after they have traveled to much more distant worlds.

Wells used neither guns nor rockets to carry his voyagers across space. His scientist, Cavor, invented a wonderful substance which acted as a screen to gravity—the force which gives us our weight—just as a piece of dark glass can screen out light. Anything surrounded by this "Cavorite" lost its weight and, since the Earth could no longer hold it down, went sailing up into the sky. So Wells' spaceship was simply a large sphere entirely covered with Cavorite screens which could be opened or closed as required. If you wanted to go to the Moon, you opened the screen on the Moonward side of the sphere, and you rose in that direction. It was as simple as that!

Sad to say, anyone who devotes his life to the search for Cavorite will be starting on a wild-goose chase. It is quite easy to show that a gravity screen of this kind could not possibly exist. One day, perhaps, we *may* be able to control gravity in some fashion. But it will need a great deal of power to do so, and certainly would not be managed simply by opening and closing the blinds!

That need not worry us unduly, for we do not require any wonderful new inventions to carry us to the planets. The tool for the job has been known for over seven hundred years, since the Chinese made the first gunpowder rockets around the year 1200. But until recent times, the rocket was little more than a firework, its main practical use being for shooting rescue lines to shipwrecked mariners. During the 19th century it was employed as a weapon for a short period, but when more accurate guns were built, war rockets soon became obsolete. They played no important part at all in the First World War.

There are many reasons why interest in the rocket revived from 1920 onward. In the first place, man had now conquered the air and so achieved one of his ancient yearnings. Flying had always been considered impossible by most people: when the Wright brothers started to make their first short aerial hops in 1903, newspaper editors refused to print the story because they *knew* it couldn't be true! Yet by the 1920's, airplanes were flying all over the world. After the air, the next step could only be— space.

But space was airless, so some new form of engine was needed, an engine that would carry *all* its fuel and wouldn't have to "push" against something outside it in order to move forward. An airplane can reach only a certain height, usually a dozen miles at the very most, because it depends on the atmosphere around it in several ways. In the first place, the fuel it carries could not burn without the oxygen in the air; the motor would "suffocate," just as you would under the same conditions. The wings would have nothing to work upon, for it is the air flowing around them that supports the plane. And, of course, the controls would be equally useless. It makes very little difference whether the aircraft is driven by propellers or jets; its ceiling is strictly limited owing to the thinness of the upper atmosphere. Airplanes not using rockets have flown higher than 20 miles only twice: the record is 21.5 miles, reached by a Russian pilot in 1961.

Balloons, floating in the air like a cork on water, can do considerably better than this. If they are carrying only small loads, they can reach heights of 30 miles before the air can no longer support them. At this altitude, the air is so thin that, even if it were compressed a hundredfold, it would not be as dense as it is down here at sea level. Beyond this region, only rockets can ever fly.

Although, as we have already seen, Jules Verne knew this back in 1865, few scientists gave the rocket any serious thought until the end of the First World War. Even then, it was first looked upon merely as a way of sending automatic instruments far above the Earth, as had already been done with balloons. The idea that it could carry men as well was, for a long time, rather too fantastic too accept, but by 1930 nearly everyone knew that if we ever *did* succeed in building spaceships, they would be rocket-propelled.

By now, the words *rocket* and *spaceship* have almost become interchangeable. First through science fiction stories and films, then through newspaper headlines, the world grew accustomed to the notion of rocket-propelled spaceships traveling through space. Two of Hollywood's most elegant spaceships, dating from the era before actual space travel began, can be seen in Plates 3 and 4. As it turned out, the spaceships we send to the moon look rather less streamlined than these, and those which will take us on really long voyages to the planets will be very different indeed; but our spaceships, like those of science fiction, are all rocket-powered.

The man who did most to draw attention to the possibilities of rocket flight was a Rumanian-born mathematician, Professor Hermann Oberth (Plate 5), who had become interested in space travel while he was still a student in the early years of the 20th century. In his books he was able to show that there was nothing impossible about space flight, *if* one could use the right sort of fuel and carry enough of it. Oberth did little actual experimenting; nearly all his work was with pencil and paper. However, he fired the imaginations of the young German space enthusiasts, such as the teen-aged Wernher von Braun.

Something quite similar happened in Russia. As early as 1883 , an obscure provincial schoolteacher named Konstantin Tsiolkovski had begun to work out the basic principles of space flight. In 1903—the very year the Wright brothers flew—he published a paper explaining exactly how a rocket could be used to escape from the Earth.

Unfortunately, Tsiolkovski's work was almost unknown, even in Russia, until the 1920's; thereafter he was widely acclaimed, and provided an inspiration to many of his countrymen. They set out to achieve his ideas—and succeeded. It is a complete fallacy to believe, as many Americans still do, that the Russians built their rockets with the help of captured German engineers. Though they received a small amount of help, it was not vital to them. The United States received far more!

Before any invention can progress from a sketch on paper to a machine that actually works, many tests and experiments are needed. The laws of aeronautics had been known for almost a hundred years before the Wrights made their first successful flying machine. Conquering space would be an even more difficult task, and the first step that had to be taken was to make more efficient and more powerful rockets than had ever been built before.

And so we come to a chapter of history which opened in the years when Hitler was making himself master of Germany, and which ended a little more than ten years later, in the dark war years of the 1940's, when the first V-2's began to climb toward the frontiers of space.

2

From Firework to V-2

There are two different kinds of rocket, one of which has been in existence for more than 700 years, while the second was born just before the Second World War. Everyone knows the old-fashioned variety which goes soaring skyward in such numbers on Guy Fawkes Day in Great Britain and Independence Day in the United States. This is the familiar powder rocket, consisting simply of a hollow tube packed with a type of slow-burning gunpowder. There is a small nozzle at the end of the tube, made in the cheap cardboard variety merely by pinching the walls of the cylinder together. As the powder burns, a great volume of gas is produced, which comes rushing out of the nozzle at a high speed and drives the rocket upward. The rocket was, in fact, the first jet-propelled vehicle! And although we will spend some time later seeing exactly how this method of propulsion works, it might be a good idea to correct one very common mistake right now. The rocket does *not*, as so many people still imagine, move forward because the hot exhaust gases "push against the air behind." In fact, it works much better when there is *no* air behind—in other words, out in space.

The powder rocket, though it is so simple to manufacture, has a number of serious disadvantages. In the first place, there is no control over the thrust or push produced once burning has started. How inconvenient it would be to have a car which ran at full speed until the fuel tank was empty, and had no throttle at all!

Secondly, such solid-fuel rockets, as they are called, are usually very inefficient. Explosives like gunpowder can produce impressive bangs, but they actually contain a good deal less energy than the same weight of liquid fuels such as gasoline or alcohol.

To make better rockets, therefore, it was necessary to abandon the old design and the old propellants, and to develop real "rocket motors" which would burn liquids pumped into them from outside. Such rockets could be started or stopped as required, and by the use of properly designed nozzles and combustion chambers much better performances could be obtained than were ever possible with the old powder rockets.

The original type of rocket is, however, by no means extinct, altogether apart from its use as a firework. The vast majority of rocket weapons now employed in warfare, such as those launched from aircraft, are of this kind. The Polaris and Minuteman missiles of the United States also are solid-fueled. However, solid-fuel rockets play only a minor role in space exploration, and, since that situation is unlikely to change in the immediate future, we will not refer to them again. The great rockets that have carried astronauts to the Moon were powered by liquid fuels.

The first liquid-propellant rocket motors were built in the United States soon after the First World War by Dr. Robert H. Goddard (1882-1945), a brilliant but very retiring scientist (Plate 6). He published hardly any of his results, probably because of the wild newspaper comments which always followed accounts of rocket experimenting in his day.

Consequently, very little was known about Goddard's work, and experiments in Europe went on independently. The men carrying them out were a group of young Germans with very little money but great enthusiasm. Just outside Berlin, during the years 1927 to 1933, they built numerous small rocket motors which they first tested on the ground and then flew to heights of a few thousand feet, landing them again by parachute.

These experiments attracted a great deal of publicity, but much more important was the fact that they really established the basis of rocket engineering as we know it today, and provided the training for the men who were later, with the support of the German Army, to build the V-2.

It is a sad fact that only in time of war can scientists obtain backing for their more imaginative ideas. Radar, jet propulsion, atomic energy, and rockets might not have reached their present stage of development even in a hundred years. But at the great German research center of Peenemünde, on the shores of the Baltic, the pressure of military needs enabled the rocket to grow from a toy to a giant missile taller than a house—all in less than ten years. And it was the "cold war" rivalry of the United States and the Soviet Union, about a decade later, that led to the development of the technology that put space satellites into orbit and sent astronauts to the Moon.

The man who directed the V-2 project, Dr. Wernher von Braun (Plate 7), had become fascinated by the idea of space travel while he was a boy, and had worked with the German Rocket Society when he was still in his teens. Next to radar and the atom bomb, the V-2 was the greatest scientific achievement of the war. It could carry a ton of explosives more than 200 miles in less than five minutes.

Most of the V-2's flight was unpowered: it built up speed by the thrust of its rocket motor for the first minute, and thereafter coasted under its momentum for the rest of the journey, which lasted another four minutes. Since most of its flight path was at altitudes of over twenty miles, there was practically no air resistance to slow it down.

This brings us to a most important point. When we start anything moving here on Earth—a car, a boat, a stone rolling along the ground—friction very quickly brings it to rest. To keep the object on the move, we have to continue to apply some force.

This is not true in space, where there is no friction of any kind. The planets move round the Sun at speeds of many thousands of miles an hour—but there's nothing to slow them down, so they'll keep on traveling forever. In the same way, a rocket could travel through space for eternity without using a drop of fuel beyond that which was needed to launch it from Earth.

However, the V-2's speed of 3,500 mph was far too low to let it escape from Earth's grip. After a few minutes, the steady pull of gravity was able to check its upward flight. Like any other object thrown up into the air, the V-2 had to fall back eventually, following the curve which mathematicians call a parabola. By adjusting the speed which the rocket reached, its range could be varied, just as one can throw a ball for varying distances by altering the force of one's throw.

Dr. von Braun was only 30 when the first V-2 was launched after several hundred million dollars had been spent on its development. Even then more than 60,000 alterations to the design had to be made before it could be used in military operations. These figures give only a slight indication of the cost of large-scale rocket research. The expenses of the American lunar program of the 1960's ran to about 25 billion dollars.

The V-2 (Plates 8 and 9) was a tremendous advance over anything that had gone before. Before it could be built, many smaller rockets had been fired to test the thousands of different devices which were incorporated in the final missile. For although the rocket motor itself seems such a simple arrangement, many complicated accessories are needed to ensure that it works properly (Figure 1).

First, of course, are the tanks for the propellants. The fuel used in the V-2 was alcohol, and the rocket carried no less than four tons of this in a large aluminum tank. But a fuel won't burn by itself; it needs oxygen. Other types of engines get their oxygen from the surrounding air; the rocket, however, carries its supply along with it. The V-2 therefore had a second tank holding nearly five tons of liquid oxygen. (Solid-fuel rockets also contain oxygen, but it is combined chemically in such nonliquid substances as saltpeter or potassium nitrate.)

The next problem was to get the alcohol and oxygen from the tanks into the motor where they would be burned. This might seem a rather easy matter—until one realizes

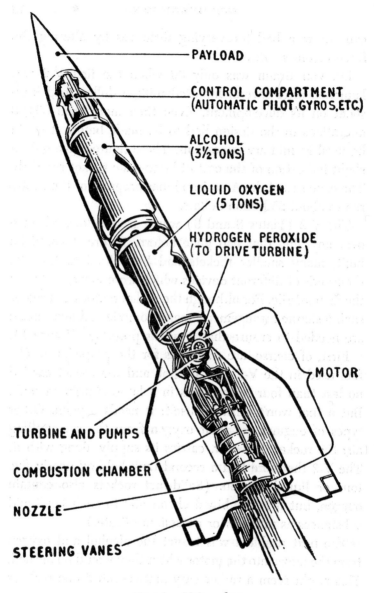

PAYLOAD

CONTROL COMPARTMENT
(AUTOMATIC PILOT GYROS, ETC.)

ALCOHOL
(3½ TONS)

LIQUID OXYGEN
(5 TONS)

HYDROGEN PEROXIDE
(TO DRIVE TURBINE)

MOTOR

TURBINE AND PUMPS

COMBUSTION CHAMBER

NOZZLE

STEERING VANES

Fig. 1. V-2 rocket.

the rate at which a large rocket uses up its propellants. In the case of the V-2, the rate was *one ton every eight seconds*. Even that seems trifling compared with the fantastic rate at which today's giant rockets consume fuel: the huge Saturn 5 that sent Neil Armstrong and his two companions to the Moon in 1969 used *fifteen* tons *every* second. Building pumps to handle such a rate of flow was in itself a major engineering achievement. The V-2 pumps were driven by a little steam turbine which could be held in both hands, yet developed over 500 horsepower. A Saturn 5 also uses turbine-driven pumps, but the turbines must generate over 300,000 horsepower. This is twice the engine power of the largest ocean liner.

The steam needed to drive the V-2's turbine was produced in a very ingenious manner. You may know the chemical called hydrogen peroxide, which is widely used for bleaching. The variety sold in shops is really 95% water, which is just as well. For hydrogen peroxide breaks down very readily into oxygen and water, producing a large amount of heat as it does so. You can see this even with the weak household variety, which continually gives off bubbles of oxygen. The pure substance, however, decomposes rapidly when certain chemicals are added to it, generating so much heat that large quantities of steam are produced. It was this steam that was used to drive the turbine pumps of the V-2.

The heart of any rocket vehicle is, of course, the motor itself, which has to handle enormous forces and very high temperatures. The V-2 motor, though it was only five feet long, produced energy equal to the electrical needs of a large city. This meant that it had to be very carefully designed, for if anything went wrong there would almost certainly be a tremendous explosion. True, the V-2 designers wanted to produce an explosion—but at the end of the flight, not at the beginning!

A modern rocket motor consists of two main parts: the combustion chamber and the nozzle. The propellants—alcohol and liquid oxygen for the V-2, kerosene and liquid oxygen for the first stage of the Saturn 5—are pumped into the combustion chamber and ignited either electrically or by some other means. Once the propellants have started to burn, the motor will continue to run as long as fuel and oxygen are pumped into it. Because of the heat produced, the liquids one starts with are turned instantly into huge volumes of gas (mostly steam and carbon dioxide), which rush out through the nozzle.

The job the nozzle does is, to put it rather roughly, to see that the hot exhaust gases leave the rocket all moving in the same direction and at the greatest possible speed. The more efficiently the nozzle does its work, the greater the thrust or "push" that the rocket will produce.

The V-2 motor, a colossus in its own time, gave a thrust of nearly 30 tons. This is dwarfed by the Saturn 5, which is equipped with five engines having a total thrust of 3,750 tons. It is sometimes hard to realize that such enormous forces can be produced by nothing more than a jet of gas, yet, when one considers what damage gales and hurricanes can do, it is perhaps not so surprising. In the fiercest of hurricanes, the wind speed may exceed 100 mph—but the speed of the gases coming from a modern rocket motor is 8,000 mph.

A large rocket is of no use unless you can make it go in

the required direction, and the V-2 was not merely aimed like a gun but was actually steered in flight just like an airplane. Although it had fins, these were useless in the thin air of the upper atmosphere and a new method of steering had to be devised. Fixed to the body of the V-2 were two pairs of little vanes or rudders lying in the path of the exhaust gases. Normally these vanes were edge on, as it were, to the exhaust. If they were tilted, however, the pressure of the gases against them would slue the rocket around, and so it could be steered in any desired direction—up or down, right or left. These were operated by an automatic mechanism carried aboard the V-2. In today's rockets, steering is done by tilting the entire motor or motor group—just as one swings the outboard motor on a small boat. This is a more complicated method than using vanes, but it is also more effective.

Tanks—pumps—motor—these are the basic units of any modern liquid-propellant rocket. In addition, there are many valves and seals, and masses of piping, to make sure that the various liquids flow in the right directions and at the correct rates. There are also intricate and sophisticated control devices and automatic pilots. Some of these are operated from self-contained electronic "brains" in the rocket itself, and others are controlled by radio impulses from ground stations. It is not at all surprising, therefore, that a spacegoing rocket costs millions of dollars.

The first V-2 was launched in 1942, but fortunately for England another two years were needed before it was ready to be used. Even then it still had many flaws, and half the V-2's fired never reached their targets. The

1,115 which did reach London killed about 3,000 people.

To understand how the V-2 operated, let's go back for a moment to the spring of 1945, to the closing days of the Second World War. The place is Holland, not far from The Hague. You're looking along an avenue of trees stretching into the distance on either side of a narrow lane. It's a peaceful, rustic scene, and there is absolutely no sign of life.

Yet there has been heavy traffic here—there are broad tire marks everywhere—and what are those curious concrete slabs set in the ground at regular intervals? You look around you—and *now* you understand why the place is so deserted. For, standing on one of the concrete slabs, so close that you can see the slight wrinkles in its metal skin, is a V-2 waiting to be launched. The alcohol and oxygen tanks have already been filled: the tire marks were made by the heavy tank trucks when they drove away. In a hidden dugout close at hand, the launching crew is waiting for the signal to fire.

There's a sudden rumbling roar as vapor gushes from the rocket's nozzle. The pumps have started; alcohol and oxygen are pouring into the combustion chamber. A moment later, with a screaming thunder that seems to shake earth and sky, ignition comes and flame bursts forth from the base of the rocket. Yet it does not move: the motor is still throttled back and the thrust is not yet powerful enough to lift the missile.

A few seconds later, when the firing commander is satisfied that everything is working properly, he switches to full power. The rocket lifts from its pad, while flames splash around it in all directions. It's going up—oh, so slowly and gracefully—balanced on that roaring, white-hot pillar of gas. The slow, steady rise is the most surprising thing about the launch; it almost looks as if the rocket is on an invisible elevator. But it gains speed quickly—already it's a thousand feet up, accelerating away from Earth more rapidly than anything ever fell *toward* it under gravity. And now it's dwindling into the sky, climbing almost vertically, but veering just a little to the west—toward London, more than two hundred miles away. . . .

If you were in that rocket, what would you see and hear? You'd leave most of the sound behind you; you'd see the Earth snatched away, the woods and fields shrink behind, the landscape widen, towns and cities and coastline dwindle below, clouds whip past and be gone in an instant. Sixty seconds after takeoff, hurled upward by more than 600,000 horsepower, the rocket would be moving at a mile a second, its fuel tanks almost empty. Nine tons of alcohol and oxygen have raced through its motor in just over a minute.

Now the motor's cutting out—it's done its job. For the rest of the journey, the rocket will be moving under gravity alone, just as a shell does when it has left the gun.

We're now 20 miles above the Earth, now climbing no longer vertically but at an angle of 45 degrees, for the automatic pilot in the control compartment has done its work. The sound you hear coming through the rocket's walls is the thin air rushing past at 3,500 mph. As we soar toward the edge of the atmosphere even this will die away into the utter and everlasting silence of space.

Look at the sky above. It's quite black, for there's no

more air to scatter the sunlight. The familiar blue vault
of heaven is already far below us. Overhead, the brighter
stars are shining, even though it's daytime and the sun is
visible down there in the south.

Forty miles up, we're still rising, though more slowly
now. Spread out beneath us like a giant map lie all the
countries of western Europe, curving down to the misty
horizon 600 miles away. A storm is coming in from the
Atlantic, and we can see its cloud banks covering Wales
and Ireland with a gleaming white layer. To the south,
we can look across Switzerland far down into Italy, but
the only sign of the Alps is a bright patch that might easily
be mistaken for cloud. We are so high that even the greatest mountains are flattened into the landscape.

And now the rocket has reached the peak of its flight.
Sixty miles above the Earth, halfway across the North
Sea, it has ceased to climb, and for a brief instant it is
traveling horizontally. If it could maintain this speed and
height it could cross the Atlantic in less than an hour—but
already it is beginning to drop down the long slope to
London, still a hundred miles away. And as it falls, it
starts to gain speed once more.

The million and a half square miles we could see from
the highest point of the flight are slowly contracting as
we sink again to ground. Behind us, central Europe has
dropped below the horizon's edge; ahead, only part of
Ireland is still visible. Yet, though the rocket is falling, its
nose is still pointing to the stars overhead. Since there's
practically no air resistance to act on the fins, there's
nothing to make the missile turn into the direction of flight.
At the moment, indeed, it's actually moving *sideways*

through space. Not until it enters the lower atmosphere again will the air rushing past veer the rocket around toward its target.

Only 40 miles to go, and the speed is mounting rapidly. Listen! Instead of the silence of space, around us now is a faint whistle of air, rising second by second to a screaming roar. We're coming back into the stratosphere, far more swiftly than we rose through it on the way up. The pressure of air on the fins is swinging the rocket around, aiming it toward the city's heart. The air resistance is swiftly rising; like a meteor, the rocket is becoming heated by the tremendous friction. Already the steel nose is glowing red-hot . . . less than ten miles to go now . . .

And so, at three times the speed of sound, the first of the giant rockets descended upon London on September 8, 1944. The V-2 was developed as a weapon of war, yet the knowledge and the experience that were gathered during its building set our feet firmly on the road to space.

3

How the Rocket Works

We have now had a look at the history of the rocket, and have some idea of the elaborate machinery that went into the pioneering V-2. However, we are not interested in the use of rockets as weapons, but as vehicles to take men into the airless reaches of space. So, before we go any further, let's make sure we understand why it is that the rocket, unlike all other forms of propulsion, can still work when no atmosphere surrounds it.

All forms of movement are the result of pushing or pulling on something. When you walk, your feet push against the ground. If the ground were perfectly smooth so that you could get no grip on it, movement would be impossible—as anyone who has tried walking on ice will agree! Locomotives and automobiles depend for their movement on the friction of the wheels against whatever supports them: the rails or the highway surface. Without this friction, the wheels would spin around but the vehicles would get nowhere.

Ships and propeller-driven aircraft rely on screws which can act on the medium around them, water in one case, air in the other. With no air or water, they too would be helpless.

Yet a rocket out in space has nothing around it; in fact, it is in a better vacuum than we can make on Earth. So how can it possibly move if, as it seems, it has "nothing to push against"?

The answer is really quite simple. The rocket carries with it something that it *can* push against: its own fuel!

Imagine that you were out in space, and that some large, heavy object was floating beside you. If you could brace yourself against this object and then give it a good kick, you would move off in one direction and the object would move off in the other. It would have given you something to push against; moreover, if its weight (or strictly speaking, its mass) were the same as yours, it would move in one direction at exactly the same speed as you moved in the other.

Now picture a rocket in the same sort of situation. It's a massive body, and most of it consists of fuel. (The 3,200-ton Saturn 5 carries fifteen times its empty weight in propellants; with no fuel on board it weighs just a little over 200 tons.) This fuel is pumped into the combustion chamber, where it burns violently and continuously. As a result, the burnt gases are "kicked" down the nozzle at thousands of miles an hour. It's that kick, *inside* the rocket motor, which moves the whole rocket forward. As long as there's fuel to burn, it will continue to gain speed.

What happens to the burnt exhaust gases once they have left the rocket doesn't matter in the least. The only effect that any surrounding air could have would be to slow down the escaping gases and thus to *reduce* the thrust of the motor. The rocket's performance, therefore, steadily improves as it climbs out of the atmosphere.

Once we understand how the rocket works, we can see that the speed it is capable of reaching (forgetting for the moment about the effects of gravity and air resistance) depends on two things. The most important of these is the speed with which the gases come out of the nozzle—the exhaust velocity, to give it its proper name. If you could double a rocket's exhaust velocity, you'd enable the rocket itself to reach twice as great a speed.

The other important factor is, of course, the actual amount of propellants the rocket can carry. The larger we can make the tanks in relation to the rest of the rocket— motor, controls, structure, skin, *and* cargo or payload—the greater its final speed when all the fuel is burnt. The most advanced models of the V-2 were only about four times as heavy when full of propellants as when empty. Today, as just noted, we have achieved a far more efficient fifteen-to-one ratio in the Saturn 5. Rockets, therefore, differ from all other forms of transport in this respect. The weight of the gasoline in an automobile is only a very small fraction of the vehicle's total weight. Even for a heavily loaded long-distance bomber, the fuel weight will rarely be more than half the aircraft's total weight. The rocket, of course, has the disadvantage of having to carry along not only its fuel but the oxygen to burn it in as well. Still, the handicap is worth it, for it gives the rocket the freedom of space.

There's still another very important respect in which rockets differ from the forms of transport we use on Earth. Automobiles, locomotives, and aircraft travel at a fairly constant speed, with their motors running all the time. Partly for reasons of fuel economy, rockets operate on a very different principle.

We have already seen that the V-2's launched against

England ran their motors only for the first minute of their flight. That was as long as the fuel lasted—but at the end of that time the great missiles had gained enough speed to coast the remainder of the journey, which lasted another four minutes.

The same sort of thing happens on space voyages, except that the difference in times is much more striking. A Saturn 5—firing its engines in several stages—burns fuel for less than five minutes altogether of its flight away from Earth. In that short time it acquires sufficient speed to coast, silently and effortlessly, without using any more fuel, on a 70-hour journey to the Moon. With very little extra energy we send planetary probes on voyages to Mars and Venus lasting many months.

When an aircraft designer makes plans for an airplane with a certain range, he has to make sure that there's enough fuel to keep the motors running for the whole length of the trip—and with something to spare. He's concerned, then, with endurance or flying time. A rocket or spaceship designer, however, is chiefly worried about the speed his vehicle will reach when it has burnt all its propellants—and the quicker it burns them the better, because then it won't have to carry along any needless weight. For any given flight or mission, there's a certain critical speed. Once the rocket has reached this, it doesn't matter that its fuel tanks are empty. If it started off in the right direction, it will cover the rest of the distance automatically under its own momentum and the influence of gravity.

The V-2 could never have gone to the Moon, because

its speed was not great enough. A rocket that merely has to escape from the gravity pull of Earth, without doing anything else—like landing on another planet—must reach a speed of no less than 25,000 miles an hour, or seven miles a second, before power is cut off. The V-2 attained a top speed of about one mile a second. Therefore rockets that traveled seven times as fast as the V-2 had to be developed before we could expect to send anything to neighboring worlds.

The solution to this problem came by means of what is known as the step, or multistage, rocket. A single-stage rocket such as the V-2 must carry all the way to its destination its huge empty fuel tanks and other structures that were necessary to it only when it was fully fueled. The rocket would have been far more effective if all this bulk could have been thrown away when no longer needed. This can be managed by arranging things so that one rocket carries another smaller one on its nose. The two separate as soon as the larger rocket has exhausted its fuel; the smaller missile, starting with a considerable initial speed and using its own fuel, can quickly reach even higher velocities. Indeed, *if* you could build a rocket with enough stages, there would be almost no limit to the final speed you could reach with the last and smallest stage, when all the others had dropped off. In practice, three stages are about the most we can economically expect to use.

The famous fable of the eagle and the wren illustrates the step principle perfectly. The wren, you may remember, boasted that it could fly higher than the eagle. It proved this by hiding in the eagle's feathers, waiting until the giant bird had exhausted itself in reaching its ceiling, and then flying on by itself to achieve victory, having done no work at all for most of the way.

The Saturn 5 that carried the Apollo astronauts to the Moon was an example of a multistage rocket. Its first stage, known as the S-IC, contained 2,200 tons of propellants—kerosene and liquid oxygen. At launching, the five tremendous motors of the S-IC thundered for two minutes, developing a 3,750-ton thrust, more than enough to lift the huge rocket from Cape Kennedy to the borders of Earth's atmosphere, some 30 miles up. Now empty, the S-IC was jettisoned and fell away. The five small engines of the second stage, termed the S-II, began to fire. This stage held 460 tons of liquid oxygen and a special high-energy fuel, liquid hydrogen. The Moon-bound spaceship swiftly gained in speed and altitude. In a short while the second stage consumed all its fuel and a small explosive charge cut it loose. The very much smaller rocket now was reduced to its third stage, the S-IVB, and the payload—the Apollo spacecraft itself. A brief burst of power from the S-IVB's single motor, fueled with liquid hydrogen and liquid oxygen, took the astronauts still higher, to an altitude of 115 miles above the Earth. There the engine cut off. This was the opportunity to halt the outward flight while the astronauts carried out whatever maneuvers were needed to prepare for the next phase of their journey. The three-stage boost had, step by step, driven the spacecraft to a speed of 17,500 miles an hour. That velocity placed the astronauts in orbit around the Earth. They could remain at their 115-mile altitude for weeks, if necessary, "parked," continuously circling the Earth, neither falling back to our world nor continuing on to the Moon.

When the voyagers were ready to proceed, they used the remaining fuel in the S-IVB to break out of their "parking" orbit and head Moonward. This last surge of power raised the spacecraft's speed to the required 25,000 miles an hour, the escape velocity needed to get free of Earth's pull. Now the burned-out third stage met the same fate as its two predecessors and, unhindered by useless bulk, the little Apollo vehicle began its history-making 70-hour glide toward the Moon.

The development of the multistage rocket was one of the key achievements along the path from the V-2 to the conquest of space. Another was the production of fuels with far greater energy content than the V-2's alcohol, such as the special type of kerosene and the liquid hydrogen used in the Saturn 5. Rocket engines became more efficient as their combustion chamber pressures were raised from less than 300 to more than 1,000 pounds per square inch.

Even so, our present chemically-propelled rockets are still terribly inefficient. They are good enough to take us to other worlds, but they are extremely expensive to operate, and probably always will be. The trouble is that 99% of the fuel in a big rocket is expended in merely lifting other fuel; the remaining 1% could do all the work that is really needed. If we had a virtually weightless energy source, space flight would be much cheaper.

It's at this point that someone always asks the question: "What about atomic power? Look at the energy that's released when an H-bomb goes off! Surely there's enough there to drive spaceships anywhere you please!"

Well, so there is. The *energy* is certainly there, all right. But an enormous explosion is no use to us; we want a steady, controllable push, which is just what the H-bomb doesn't give.

Still, there's good reason to think that spaceships eventually will be driven by atomic energy. We've seen that the only way we can create a thrust in the vacuum of space is by throwing something away from the spaceship as rapidly as possible, thus producing a reaction, or recoil. We'd get exactly the same recoil whether we used chemical energy or nuclear energy to blast the exhaust gases out of the rocket nozzle.

Besides its use in the bomb, nuclear energy can be liberated at any desired rate in atomic piles or reactors. An atomic reactor consists, basically, of bars of uranium or other radioactive elements arranged in a kind of grid; when operating they develop great quantities of heat. The commercial power plants that now are in such widespread use employ this heat, in the form of steam, to drive turbines that generate electricity.

In theory, all that one has to do to build an atomic rocket is to construct a high-temperature reactor and blow hydrogen through it. The gas would expand as it grows hot, and could then be allowed to escape through a nozzle to create a propulsive thrust. Unfortunately, there are some serious technical problems, such as the need to shield the rocket's passengers and instruments against the dangerous radiation the reactor gives off. Nevertheless, nuclear rockets of this type have now been built and successfully tested on the ground (projects ROVER and NERVA). Used in the upper stages of a Saturn V, they could double—at least—its payload, and would make possible manned flights to Mars.

However, there's still another way of using nuclear energy for spaceships, and this may prove to be a lot easier. It's a device which has been called an "electric rocket." Instead of using heat to make gases expand out of a nozzle, the idea is to drive the rocket with high-velocity electric fields. A very small example of this can be found in the familiar cathode-ray tube of the TV set. Here a stream of electrons, moving at a very great speed, is produced by high voltages in the tube. Though electrons are very tiny, they have *some* mass, and so this stream causes a minute recoil, far too small to be detected in the ordinary way. There is no danger that this stream of tiny electrical bullets, as it paints its pictures on the screen, will ever drill a hole through the glass of your TV set.

Yet tests—including some during actual space flights—have shown that this principle could be developed to obtain useful thrusts for spaceships. The necessary electric fields could be produced by atomic energy. Extremely high exhaust velocities have been achieved, but the thrust levels are feeble—mere fractions of a pound. Naturally, such devices are useless for the escape from Earth, but once beyond Earth's pull they could be used to drive a rocket for days or weeks. A rocket's speed increases constantly as its engine continues to fire, so one of these low-thrust long-firing electric propulsion systems could eventually impart very high speeds to a space-going vehicle, while chemical rockets remained in use for takeoffs and landings.

This seems a good place to stop and sum up the conclusions we've now reached. Here they are:

First, rockets work better in airless space than they do in an atmosphere.

Second, most of the mass of a rocket consists of its propellants, which are burned in a very short time compared with the total time of flight. Once the rocket has reached the necessary speed to make any trip, the motor can be switched off, and it's then only a matter of waiting until the destination is reached.

Third, the speeds needed for even the easiest of interplanetary voyages are very great, as it takes 25,000 mph merely to escape from the gravity pull of Earth.

Fourth, such high speeds can be attained by step or multistage rockets, each stage being discarded after it has done its work.

Fifth, improvements will continue to be made in the design and fueling of chemical rockets, but sooner or later atomic energy will be used for spaceships.

4

Above the Atmosphere

When the Second World War ended in 1945, and the results of German rocket research were revealed, aeronautics made a great leap forward—and the new science of *astronautics* was born. For the first time it had become possible to send objects beyond the atmosphere, as the V-2, with its ceiling of 115 miles, was just able to reach space itself.

What, however, do we mean by "space"? As we go higher and higher in the atmosphere, the air rapidly gets thinner—but there is no point at which one can say that it actually ends. Twenty miles up, it's a hundred times thinner than at sea level. That is still quite dense enough to have a considerable effect on bodies moving at high speeds. But 120 miles up, the air is less than *one hundred millionth* of its sea level density. To get some idea of what this means, imagine that you let a thimbleful of ordinary air expand into a vacuum until it takes up as much volume as the average house. The resulting gas would be about as dense as the atmosphere 120 miles up! For all practical purposes, therefore, we can say that at such heights we are "in space."

After the fall of Germany, the United States seized more than 100 complete V-2's, plus blueprints, spare parts, and test equipment. They also brought some 150 German rocket scientists—Wernher von Braun included—to the States.

With this nucleus, the postwar American rocket research program began at the White Sands Proving Ground in New Mexico.

The United States had already developed some small solid-fuel high-altitude rockets of its own. The first, in 1944, was the Private; it was followed in 1945 by a slender, 16-foot-long rocket known as the WAC-Corporal, which reached heights of 40 miles. Two years later the Aerobee emerged—18 feet long and capable of carrying a 154-pound payload to a height of 70 miles. With these rockets and the captured V-2's, the White Sands group obtained information about the temperature and pressure in the upper atmosphere, as well as valuable data concerning the mysterious cosmic rays which continually bombard us from space. Each rocket carried low-powered radio transmitters which automatically sent back to ground stations the readings of the instruments on board—a technique known as "telemetering."

In February, 1949, a WAC-Corporal boosted by a V-2 soared 252 miles above Earth's surface—man's first genuine stab into the darkness of space. The shot made history for another reason: it was the first firing of a large-scale two-stage rocket. The V-2 provided the power for the first 20 miles of the climb; when it exhausted its propellants it was cut loose and fell back to Earth, and the slim WAC-Corporal began to spout flame and spurt upward on its own power, reaching an ultimate speed of 5,100 mph.

The next year, however, the United States became involved in the Korean War and in domestic problems, and the young space program moved into the background. Research continued, and new, larger rockets were built,

but progress was slow. One project that seemed doomed never to materialize was the plan, first made public in 1948, of putting an artificial satellite in orbit around the Earth.

The Earth already had one conspicuous natural satellite —the Moon—and the scientists who planned to launch artificial satellites hoped to keep them aloft by making use of the same principle that keeps the Moon from falling down. As Sir Isaac Newton showed more than 300 years ago, the Moon is held securely in its place by the same force that holds us to the Earth: gravity.

There is a common impression that at a certain height gravity disappears. That's quite untrue; Earth's gravity reaches to the remotest stars. But it gets steadily weaker with distance, and when one is a few million miles away it is so feeble that, for almost all practical purposes, it can be ignored.

Newton's law of gravitation, like most great discoveries, can be put into very simple words. It states that, as one goes away from the Earth, gravity decreases according to the square of one's distance from Earth's center. That is, doubling your distance reduces the force of gravity to a *quarter*; increasing it tenfold reduces gravity to a *hundredth*.

Every planet—every body in the universe, in fact—has a gravity of its own. Its value on any world depends on the size and mass of that world. The giant planet Jupiter has almost three times as powerful a gravity as Earth's; the Moon's gravity, on the other hand, is only a sixth of ours.

What keeps the Moon up, then?

The mutual gravity of Earth and Moon draws the two

bodies together with a force of millions of tons. If it had no movement around the Earth, the Moon would soon crash into us. But the Moon *has* such a movement, which is why it doesn't fall. It's swinging round the Earth in a great circle, moving at a speed of over 2,000 mph. As long as it maintains that speed it can never fall down.

Everyone knows that if you tie a stone at the end of a piece of string, you can set it whirling in a circle with very little effort. This is a crude working model of what happens with the Moon. Here, the pull of gravity plays the same role as the tension of the string. So the Moon's velocity saves it from falling down, and Earth's gravity prevents it from flying off into space.

If for any reason the Moon altered its distance slightly, the speed would automatically adjust itself, so there's no danger of anything suddenly going wrong. Indeed, such variations are always taking place, because the Moon's orbit is not exactly circular.

Now, there is no reason at all why the Moon should be at the particular distance it is. It could be much closer, or much farther away—as long as its speed was correctly adjusted to balance gravity at that point. To return to our stone-and-string analogy, we know that the shorter the string, the faster the stone has to be moved. The same rule applies to moons revolving around planets, and to planets revolving around the Sun. Mercury, the nearest planet to the Sun, rushes along at 30 miles a second, whereas remote Pluto, at the borders of the solar system, needs only a tenth of this speed to maintain itself in its orbit. Some planets have at least a dozen moons scattered at all sorts of distances and revolving quite happily in their various orbits. There is no law of nature stopping us from having a moon only a couple of hundred miles up, instead of one a quarter of a million miles away.

Such a moon would have to move almost ten times as quickly as the real Moon does, since gravity is much stronger so close to the Earth. But this could be managed by sending the artificial satellite into space aboard a rocket traveling at a speed of about 18,000 mph. At that speed—the so-called orbital velocity for that height—the satellite's natural tendency to keep traveling away from Earth on a straight line would be exactly balanced by the tendency of Earth's gravity to pull it back. The pull of gravity thus bends the straight line into a closed curve, and the satellite enters a permanent orbit around the Earth, unable either to continue outward or to drop back to the ground. In effect, it is forever "falling" but can never land. (Actually a satellite in orbit close to the Earth—less than 150 miles up—will gradually be slowed by contact with the fringes of the atmosphere, until, after years or perhaps centuries, its speed drops below orbital velocity and it falls to Earth. But a satellite that never enters the denser parts of the atmosphere can remain in orbit forever, as the planets themselves do.)

In 1954, Wernher von Braun declared that he could put a 15-pound satellite into orbit within two years by using the Redstone rocket, an improved version of the V-2 that he had developed for the United States Army. But when the government approved a space satellite program the following year, it chose to have the Navy create a completely new rocket, the Vanguard, as the satellite's booster.

Thus the head start provided by von Braun's years of work was wasted.

The Vanguard had its first successful test in December, 1956. It was 72 feet high, 45 inches in diameter, and weighed only 11 tons—three tons less than the V-2. Yet it was five times as powerful as the German-made rocket. Despite its efficiency, the Vanguard presented many technical problems, and all during 1957 the rocket engineers struggled to get it ready for the first satellite launching, originally scheduled for the summer of 1957, then postponed to fall, and then to early 1958. Then, on October 4, 1957, there came an astonishing announcement from the U.S.S.R.: a Soviet space satellite, called Sputnik, was now in orbit around the Earth!

The Russians had said in 1955 that they would put a satellite into orbit within two years. But the United States had not taken the claim seriously, and it was generally imagined that an American satellite would be the first to enter space. Now, though, a Soviet-made 184-pound metal moon was circling the Earth every 96 minutes, broadcasting a *beep-beep* radio message that seemed to mock the American space effort. With the launching of Sputnik, the age of space had unmistakably begun.

Less than a month later Sputnik II was in orbit. It weighed 1,120 pounds, and carried instruments for studying solar radiation and cosmic rays and two radio transmitters for reporting data to Earth. On board also was the world's first spaceship passenger: Laika, a dog, riding in an air-conditioned container.

A frantic attempt by the United States to rush a satellite

into orbit with a Vanguard rocket in December, 1957, failed embarrassingly. But von Braun's Redstone project was hurriedly revived, and on January 31, 1958, the first American satellite finally entered space: the 18-pound Explorer I, riding on the nose of von Braun's Jupiter-C rocket, the latest descendant of the original V-2.

With these first few satellites in orbit, the task of sending up such artificial moons no longer seemed so difficult; soon another Explorer circled above us, and then, at last a Vanguard satellite; and then a third Sputnik, one more Explorer, two more Vanguards, the first of the American Discoverer series, and many other types. Some of these satellites were designed as spy devices to observe events on Earth; others transmitted weather information, studied the impact of cosmic rays, relayed radio messages from one point on Earth to another, measured the output of the Sun's energy, and performed dozens of other scientific or military tasks.

Once sufficient rocket power had been attained—which meant being able to build a step-rocket whose final stage was capable of reaching the orbital velocity of 18,000 miles an hour—it became a relatively simple matter to pepper the sky with artificial satellites. Today, a satellite launching is such routine news that newspapers, if they mention it at all, put it on one of the back pages. We take this aspect of our conquest of space completely for granted. During the first decade of the space age, the United States and the Soviet Union put some 700 satellites into orbit. French, British, Italian, Australian, German, Canadian, and Japanese satellites also have gone up. The phenomenal pace of satellite launchings continues year after year; since 1954 it has averaged between two and three a week.

After the technical problems of orbiting satellites were solved, the next phase of man's invasion of space began: launching satellites that carried human passengers. The first human spacemen entered the pages of history.

5

On the Frontier of Space

Putting men into orbit was a far more complicated and risky project than launching artificial satellites. A failure in a manned launching would mean not only the loss of costly equipment but of a precious human life. Therefore, more powerful booster rockets had to be developed to improve the chances of lifting the manned satellite without mishap. Also, we could not simply thrust an astronaut into orbit and leave him there to die, as the Russians did with their space dog, Laika; we had to make provisions for his safe return from space.

Thus it was necessary to perfect foolproof rockets and control mechanisms by which the astronaut could leave his orbit and descend. The troublesome problem of reentry had to be solved, too—coping with the fierce heat generated when a fast-moving body enters our atmosphere from space. Unless we wanted to turn our astronauts into shooting stars, blazing momentarily in the sky, then falling as cinders, we needed a reliable heat shield system for the outer skin of their space capsules. And, of course, men had to be trained in new skills, so that they could control their capsules under the strange weightless conditions of space flight.

This business of weightlessness is one that very few laymen seem to understand. It is the normal condition in space, but this has nothing to do with being "beyond the pull of Earth's gravity." Indeed, as we have already seen, that pull is still powerful hundreds of thousands of miles away. Just above the atmosphere, where the first manned space capsules would be circling, it is practically as strong as it is down here at the surface. Then why should things become weightless?

To answer that, let's consider what we mean by weight. You feel a sensation of weight only when some force is pressing on you. When you stand, there is the pressure of the ground; when you sit, that of your chair. If the chair or the ground were abruptly removed, you'd feel weightless as long as you remained unsupported. Of course, you'd promptly start to fall, so the condition would last only for a very short time and would terminate painfully.

Now, suppose your chair were suddenly to start moving *upward*, as if in a high-speed elevator. You would feel a *greater* weight than normal, as long as the acceleration lasted. This is what we mean when we say that a pilot is "under several gravities": he is in an airplane accelerating so swiftly that his seat presses against him with several times the normal force. The same effect is felt by an astronaut as his rocket leaves its launching pad.

However, as soon as the rocket's motors are shut off, this pressure ceases. It doesn't matter whether the ship is near the Earth, where gravity is intense, or far out in space, where there is virtually no gravity. As soon as the rockets stop pushing the ship, the ship stops pushing on the people inside—and they float around freely and "weightlessly." This would happen inside a spaceship a few miles up as easily as in one a billion miles from Earth. As soon as the

rocket motors were switched on again, "weight" would return. How strong the feeling of weight would be would
depend *entirely* upon the rate at which the rockets were
accelerating the ship.

So there are really two kinds of "weight." The first is
the familiar kind, due to gravity. This, of course, varies
from planet to planet. A man who weighs 180 pounds
here would weigh only 30 on the Moon—but 480 on
Jupiter.

The other kind of weight is that due to acceleration,
and is the only kind that can occur aboard a spaceship
in flight.

Astronauts, therefore, had to undergo special training
so that they would be able to deal with the problems
they would encounter in the periods of heavy weight
during takeoff and landing and in the periods of weightlessness when their rockets were coasting. There was
no way that these conditions could be perfectly duplicated on Earth, but elaborate training devices provided
some clue to what was in store for them. Weightlessness
was going to be fun—floating about and being able to
fly like a bird—but there would be problems, too. Any
loose object an astronaut handled in his cabin would
drift about, getting in his way, unless carefully fastened
down. Eating, then, would pose some difficulties: liquids
would not stay in a glass, but would break into an in-
finity of tiny particles wandering freely everywhere. And
when space capsules got large enough for an astronaut
to move around in them, they would need plenty of
handrails and tethers to get where they wanted to go.

Providing a safe environment for the space traveler

was another time-consuming project. His cabin had to be completely sealed, yet it needed devices for purifying the air and for maintaining a comfortable temperature. Dried food could be carried, but the space traveler would need a water supply. This was eventually solved cleverly: the system of fuel cells used for generating electricity aboard space capsules also produced water as a by-product of the process.

Temperature control required careful thought. Space itself—being nothing—can, of course, have no temperature. But an object floating in space will have a temperature, which depends largely on the heat it picks up from the Sun. A spacecraft exposed to full sunlight would rapidly grow far too hot to live in if nothing were done to dispose of the excess heat. A space capsule in shadow —on the night side of Earth, for instance—would quickly lose its heat and freeze its occupants. Then, too, the spaceman's own body generates heat, which if it had no way of escaping from the capsule would build up rapidly to a fatal level. Excess heat therefore had to be radiated away into space by suitable cooling fins or surfaces; the capsules also were equipped with double walls for insulation and with other systems for adjusting their internal temperatures to varying external conditions.

In case of accident—if the capsule were punctured somehow, or if its control systems failed—the astronaut would need a protective spacesuit. Exposure to the vacuum of space would kill a spaceman in a minute or two from lack of oxygen. And he would naturally need a spacesuit if he intended to venture outside the protective confines of his capsule.

The development of a suitable spacesuit involved some elaborate engineering, for the suit had to do many other things besides providing oxygen. It had to be flexible, so that its occupant could move his limbs—but not so flexible that he would be spread-eagled by the internal pressure. (If you've ever blown up one of those toy balloons shaped like animals, you'll understand how air pressure can make an object rigid.) Because sound cannot be transmitted unless there is some substance— gas, solid, or liquid—to carry it, space is utterly silent and the suit had to have built-in radio communications equipment. It needed a transparent helmet that would give good visibility while shielding the wearer from the glare of sunlight.

These many design problems on the space capsule and spacesuit took years to solve. Both the United States and the Soviet Union began their man-in-space programs in the late 1950's. The American plan, Project Mercury, called for the launching of an astronaut-carrying capsule atop the new Atlas missile sometime in 1961 or 1962. However, by late 1960 it became apparent that a Russian was going to be the first man into space.

In August of that year a giant satellite, Sputnik V, went into orbit bearing two dogs, Strelka and Belka; in its 18th trip around the Earth, this satellite was slowed by a remote control command and was safely brought down to land. This was the first time living beings had been placed in orbit and recovered. Now the way was clear for a manned flight. After three more tests with dogs, the Russians sent a 27-year-old air force pilot, Major Yuri Alekseyevich Gagarin, into space on April

12, 1961, aboard the Vostok I capsule. Gargarin circled the earth one time, and, 108 minutes after his blastoff, came down unharmed. "I feel fine and I have no injuries or bruises," he said after stepping from his capsule. Man's adventure in space was under way.

The United States, unable then to match the power of the Russian rockets, sent astronaut Alan B. Shepard on a 15-minute flight three weeks later. But this was not intended as an orbital journey; Shepard climbed 100 miles into space in his Mercury capsule and immediately fell back to Earth, landing in the Atlantic. Not until the three-orbit flight of John Glenn on February 20, 1962 did the United States achieve its first true manned space voyage. As Yuri Gagarin had done, Glenn fired small rockets known as retro-rockets when the time came to end his flight. These, aimed against the direction of the space capsule's motion, slowed its speed and dropped it out of orbit. The Earth's gravity did the rest of the job of bringing the spaceship home.

By the time of Glenn's flight, the Soviet Union had already sent Gherman Titov up in Vostok II for a 17½-orbit voyage lasting more than 25 hours. And, in August, 1962, Russia staged a spectacular exploit by orbiting two of its cosmonauts on successive days: Andrian G. Nikolayev in Vostok III and Pavel Popovich in Vostok IV. They circled the globe together for 70 hours, and came down six minutes apart.

Several American and Russian space flights of fairly lengthy duration followed in 1963. One, the voyage of Vostok VI in June of that year, was notable because it carried Valentina Tereshkova, the first (and, so far, the only) woman to travel through space. Later she married a fellow Soviet cosmonaut and they have had several children.

In October, 1964, the Russians opened a new phase of manned space flight by orbiting a capsule that contained more than one passenger. The huge Voskhod I carried *three* men: Vladimir M. Komarov, Konstantin Feoktistov, and Boris Yegorov. They remained aloft for 24 hours, making a 16-orbit flight. The journey of Voskhod II in March, 1965, was even more astonishing; while cosmonaut Pavel Belyayev remained at the controls, his companion, Alexei Leonov, went out of the capsule through a hatch and, protected by his spacesuit, took a walk in space. "I saw the endless face of Earth, half of the globe," Leonov reported. Clinging to a wire rope 16 feet long, Leonov floated more than 100 miles above the world; a television camera aboard the capsule relayed the sight to Earth. "I felt absolutely free, soaring like a bird," he said.

Next, the United States returned to space with the first of its two-man Gemini flights, five days after Leonov's feat. On the second Gemini voyage, in June, 1965, astronaut Edward H. White duplicated Leonov's space walk. White spent 20 minutes outside his capsule at a height of 120 miles, and found the experience so wondrous that his fellow voyager, James A. McDivitt, had to order him several times, rather sharply, to come back into the ship. "It's the saddest moment of my life," White said when he finally reentered the capsule. (In January, 1967, he and astronauts Virgil Grissom and Roger Chaffee became the first casualties of the American space program when they were killed by a fire that swept through their capsule while they were still on the ground going through a prelaunch checkout. The first spacefarer to die in the actual course of a voyage was Russia's Vladimir Komarov, killed in April, 1967, when his parachute became tangled as he was returning from a 26-hour orbital mission.)

The planned climax of America's venture into space was Project Apollo: the voyage to the Moon. While the preliminary Mercury and Gemini test flights were being held in the mid-1960's, research proceeded on this grand enterprise.

There were three possible ways of managing a round-trip flight to the Moon. One, which can be called the "brute force" method, would have involved building a giant multistage rocket that would blast off from Earth, go to the Moon, land there, and still have a reserve of fuel large enough to allow it to leave the Moon and return to Earth. But such a rocket would have had to weigh something like 5,000 tons when first launched, most of that immense weight being fuel. Building such a monster seemed impractical. The Atlas rocket that carried the astronauts of Project Mercury into orbit had weighed a mere 130 tons, after all.

Possibility number two was the "Earth-rendezvous" method. In this, a rocket of more moderate size would carry the astronauts into orbit around the Earth, perhaps 150 miles up. Then a second rocket would be placed in orbit nearby, carrying propellants with which the Moon-bound ship could be refueled. Having taken on a fresh supply of fuel, the astronauts would start their engines, break out of Earth orbit, and head for the Moon.

This plan had many supporters, but the dangers seemed to outweigh the advantages, and in the end it was rejected in favor of the "Moon-rendezvous" method. This compromise scheme would allow the mission to be performed with a single launch from Earth. A multistage rocket, weighing about 3,000 tons at the outset of the journey would boost the astronauts into orbit around Earth, from which they could take off for the Moon as desired without further refueling (Plate 20). Upon reaching the vicinity of the Moon, they would put themselves in orbit around it. Then, while one astronaut waited in the circling ship, a smaller spacecraft that had been attached to it would detach and make a landing on the Moon, carrying two other astronauts. When they had completed their examination of the lunar surface, they would pilot their landing module back to a rendezvous with the orbiting command module, join the two vehicles once again, and blast off for home.

A great deal of work had to be done before this ambitious plan became reality. In December, 1965, astronauts Frank Borman and James Lovell, Jr., set a record by remaining in space for nearly 14 days. During this voyage they were joined by a second team of astronauts, Walter M. Schirra, Jr., and Thomas P. Stafford, who carried out the first space rendezvous, maneuvering their spacecraft within one foot of the Borman-Lovell vehicle as both capsules orbited the Earth. This showed that the rendezvous idea was a practical possibility.

Later flights in the Gemini series during 1966 gave the astronauts practice in docking and undocking their capsules—that is, in attaching them to one another in

1. Cyrano de Bergerac's "ramjet."

2. Jules Verne's space-gun.

3. *Spaceship on the Moon.*
From the motion picture *Destination Moon*, courtesy of Eagle-Lion

4. Building the spaceship.

From the motion picture *When Worlds Collide*, courtesy of Paramount Productions

5. Professor Hermann Oberth.

Photograph by A. C. Clarke

6. Professor Robert Goddard.

American Rocket Society

7. *Dr. Wernher von Braun.*
Photograph by A. C. Clarke

8. *V-2 rocket on trailer.*
Photograph by A. C. Clarke

9. *V-2 being prepared for launching at White Sands Proving Ground.*
Applied Physics Laboratory, Johns Hopkins University

10. *Space station.*
Design by Dr. Wernher von Braun

11. Space station.
Drawing by R. A. Smith

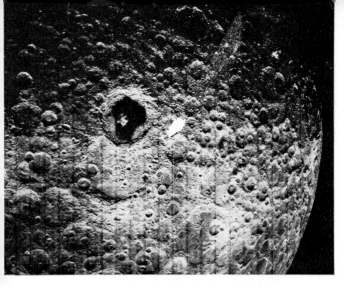

12. *Tsiolkovsky Crater, on the far side of the Moon.*
NASA

13. *Design for an Orbiting Astronomical Telescope.*
NASA
Reprinted from the December 1965 issue of *Astronautics and Aeronautics*, a publication of the American Institute of Aeronautics and Astronautics, Inc.

14. *Cloud patterns
over Earth,
photographed by ATS 1.*
Hughes Aircraft Company

15. *Tycho Crater in the Moon's
southern hemisphere.*
NASA

16. *Rendezvous with Gemini 7
as seen from Gemini 6.*
NASA

17. Telstar communications satellite.

American Institute of Aeronautics and Astronautics, Inc.

18. Earth, photographed by Lunar Orbiter V.

NASA

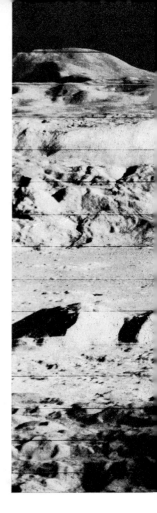

19. *Orbiter II's close-up of the crater Copernicus on the face of the Moon.*
NASA

20. *The Saturn V space vehicle used in the Apollo missions.*
North American Rockwell Corp., Space Division

21. Photo taken by Surveyor V spacecraft following soft landing in Sea of Tranquility.
Hughes Aircraft Company

22. *Astronaut Edwin E. Aldrin, Jr. descends to the surface of the Moon on the Apollo XI mission.*
NASA

23. *Astronaut Aldrin on the Moon. Astronaut Neil A. Armstrong is reflected in Aldrin's faceplate, as is the Lunar Module.*
NASA

24. *Apollo XI's Lunar Module on the Moon.*
Astronaut Aldrin can be seen in foreground.
NASA

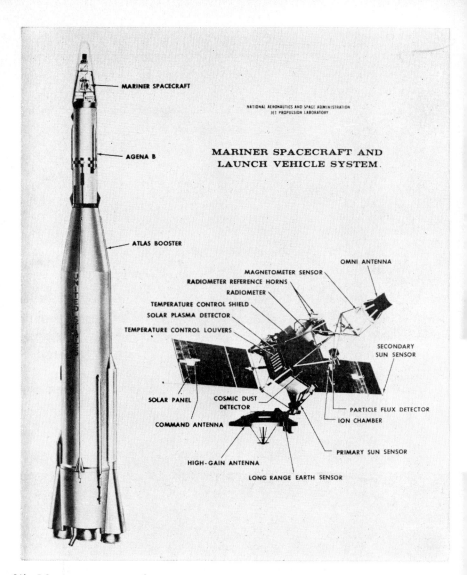

MARINER SPACECRAFT

AGENA B

ATLAS BOOSTER

NATIONAL AERONAUTICS AND SPACE ADMINISTRATION
JET PROPULSION LABORATORY

**MARINER SPACECRAFT AND
LAUNCH VEHICLE SYSTEM.**

MAGNETOMETER SENSOR
OMNI ANTENNA
RADIOMETER REFERENCE HORNS
RADIOMETER
TEMPERATURE CONTROL SHIELD
SOLAR PLASMA DETECTOR
TEMPERATURE CONTROL LOUVERS
SECONDARY
SUN SENSOR
SOLAR PANEL
COSMIC DUST
DETECTOR
PARTICLE FLUX DETECTOR
ION CHAMBER
COMMAND ANTENNA
PRIMARY SUN SENSOR
HIGH-GAIN ANTENNA
LONG RANGE EARTH SENSOR

25. *Mariner spacecraft
and launch vehicle
system.*
NASA

26. *Picture relayed
by Mariner VI shows
the rugged Martian
terrain.*
NASA

27. *Jupiter, showing Great Red Spot and satellite Ganymede and its shadow.*
Photographed with 200-inch Hale reflector, courtesy Mount Wilson and Palomar Observatories

28. *Saturn.*
Photographed with 100-inch reflector, courtesy Mount Wilson and Palomar Observatories

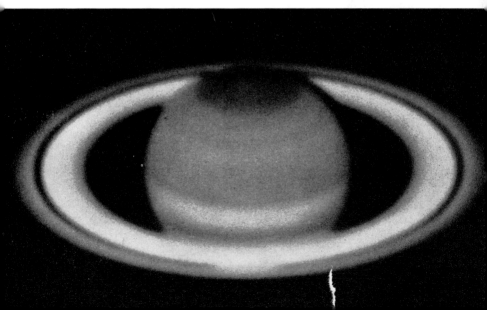

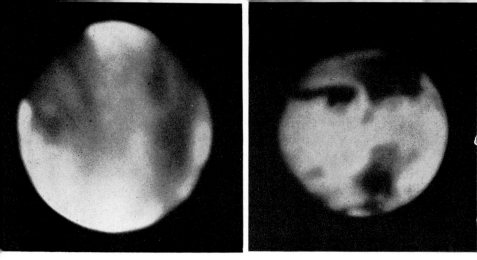

29. Mars, photographed in blue (left) and red (right) light.
Photographed with 200-inch Hale reflector, courtesy Mount Wilson and Palomar Observatories

30. Pressure Domes.
Photograph by A. C. Clarke

space and in separating them again, as would have to be done in the Apollo missions (Plate 16). Then—after a delay caused by the disastrous 1967 fire—the larger and much more complex Apollo spacecraft received its first manned test flight in October, 1968. Walter Schirra, Donn F. Eisele, and R. Walter Cunningham spent 260 hours putting it through its paces around Earth. Two months later came the landmark flight of Apollo VIII, in which men journeyed to the Moon for the first time but did not land. Blasting off on December 21, 1968, astronauts Frank Borman, James Lovell, and William Anders rode their spacecraft on a flawless 166-hour journey into orbit around the Moon. Circling the Moon 10 times in 20 hours, they hovered about 70 miles above its barren, pockmarked surface, sending back television pictures that awed and astonished the world. "The color of the Moon looks like a very whitish gray," Major Anders reported, "like dirty beach sand with lots of footprints in it."

The flight of Apollo IX followed in March, 1969. In this the fragile lunar landing module was given its first space test, orbiting the Earth. In May, the men of Apollo X tested the module in orbit around the Moon, without making an actual landing. Then came the unforgettable events of July 20, 1969—a day likely to glow forever in human history. While Michael Collins waited in lunar orbit aboard the Apollo XI command module, his colleagues Neil A. Armstrong and Edwin E. Aldrin, Jr., piloted their vessel, the Eagle, to man's first landing on the Moon's surface. "Tranquility Base here," Armstrong radioed at 4:17 in the afternoon, Eastern Daylight Time. "The Eagle has landed." About six and a half hours later he climbed out of the module to take a stroll on the Moon. Hundreds of millions of astounded Earthmen watched the whole show, live, on television—something that not even the boldest of science-fiction writers had dared to predict. Armstrong clambered down the module's ladder and, as he left it, told his worldwide audience, "That's one small step for a man, one giant leap for mankind." Then—joined shortly by Aldrin—he began to walk across the face of a world which never before had felt the weight of human feet (Plates 22, 23 and 24).

6

The Harvest of Space

The voyage of Apollo VIII and the manned lunar missions that have followed it are surely the most dramatic events of the space age thus far. But these heroic exploits are just part of the story of the conquest of space. The unmanned artificial satellites which man has put into orbit since 1957 have come to serve us in a variety of extraordinarily valuable ways.

Scores of scientific satellites have been launched, carrying instruments for hundreds of experiments. Some were extremely simple; others, like the Soviet Union's giant "Proton" satellites, nothing less than orbiting physics labs. Simply to list them would take pages, and to describe the results they have obtained has already required many volumes. At the Goddard Space Flight Center, Maryland, where information from American satellites is stored for later analysis after it has been relayed to Earth, hundreds of thousands of reels of magnetic tape are stacked in endless rows while scientists try to cope with the flood of new knowledge pouring down from the heavens.

One of the most important discoveries was made by the very first United States satellite, Explorer 1 (1958). This was the huge radiation belt, roughly doughnut-shaped, that surrounds the Earth. The inner part of the

belt consists mostly of the positive particles called protons, and is strongest at a height of about 500 miles.
In the outer zone electrons—negative particles—pre-
dominate, with their greatest intensity at 10,000 miles.
The great radiation belt—named after its discoverer, Dr.
James Van Allen—is produced by streams of electrons and
protons from the Sun which have become trapped in the
magnetic field emanating from the Earth. Once it was feared
that it would be a hazard to astronauts, but this has not
turned out to be the case.

Putting orbiting observatories into space has been a
great boon to astronomers. Even on what seems to be
a clear night, when the stars are shining brilliantly, only
a small part of the light coming from space actually
gets through our atmosphere. And what *does* get through
is distorted. If you look at one of the planets—say Mars
—through a powerful telescope, you will find that the
image is continually quivering and you can never get a
steady view.

Above the atmosphere, all this is different. Visibility
is more perfect than anything we can attain down here
on Earth. There never is night or day; the stars always
shine, right up to the blazing edge of the Sun! Observatories relaying data from space, therefore, can provide
information unavailable to Earthbound astronomers (Plate
13).

In 1962 the United States launched the Orbiting Solar
Observatory (OSO-A) satellite. It scanned the Sun for
2,000 hours, measuring and analyzing the solar radiation. Four years later the first Orbiting Astronomical
Observatory (OAO) went aloft. This was one of the most

complex satellites ever constructed, with a battery of telescopes, 440,000 separate parts, and 30 miles of wiring. Unfortunately, OAO-1 suffered a mysterious power failure and ceased to transmit information after a few hours, but OAO-2, placed in orbit in 1968, was far more successful. One of the scientists connected with this project said, as OAO-2 completed its second year of service 500 miles above the Earth, "No other observatory on the ground, or in space, to my knowledge, has contributed so much to astronomy in its first two years of operation as OAO-2." This satellite discovered a huge hydrogen cloud, a million miles in diameter, around a comet known as Tago-Sato-Kosaka; it revealed important facts about the makeup of the atmosphere of Mars; and it discovered that the hottest stars are even hotter than suspected, and are burning hydrogen more swiftly than astronomers had believed.

Weather forecasts are now made with the help of satellites that send back pictures of cloud formations covering whole continents. The first of these, Tiros (Television and Infrared Observation Satellite), went into a 400-mile-high-orbit in 1960; it was followed by nine more of its kind, then by the more advanced Nimbus and Essa satellites. As these pass overhead, ground-based weather stations can pick up the weather picture for a thousand miles around. By means of these satellites, hurricanes have been detected far out at sea hours before their existence could have been discovered in any other way. Less spectacular weather developments may also be predicted by studying the photos from space.

As far back as 1945, it was suggested that orbiting

space satellites would be ideal for television and radio transmission. The short waves used in TV will not go around the curve of the Earth, which is why our present stations have such a limited range and we have to use enormously expensive coaxial cables or relays if we want to send a TV signal over great distances. But a station up in space, looking down on an entire hemisphere, could broadcast its programs to half the planet at once. A ground station would beam the signal to the satellite, which would amplify it and rebroadcast it at greatly increased power.

The first relay satellite of this kind to go into public service was Telstar 1, launched in 1962. Because the rockets then available lacked the power to lift large payloads to very high orbits, Telstar and its immediate successors orbited fairly close to the Earth. Therefore they moved quite rapidly and stayed over any one ground station for just a few minutes at a time. As a result, they could not provide the continuous type of service needed for commercial use: it would be awkward for the ground stations to have to keep their TV antennas moving all the time in order to follow the satellite trans-mitters as they sped across the sky.

One solution might have been to set up a whole series of Telstar-type low-altitude satellites, more or less equally spaced around the world so that there was always at least one above the horizon at any given point. But a better method was available. At a certain distance from Earth—which happens to be about 22,000 miles—it would take just one day for a satellite to make its complete orbit. The Earth, of course, also takes one day to turn on its axis. This means that from our point of view the satellite would always be fixed in the sky—it would never rise or set. Once the ground antennas had been aimed in the right direction, they could be left pointing that way, and need never be moved again. Three satellites in fixed orbits of this kind would provide worldwide TV relay service. They would also make possible far more efficient radio service, and could be used as well for relaying long-distance telephone calls (Figure 2).

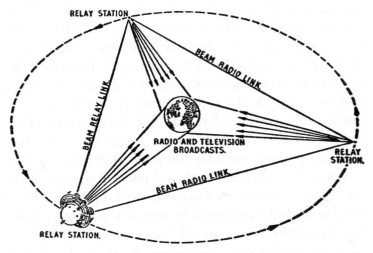

Fig. 2. Space-station relay system.

Improvements in rocket power allowed the first successful launchings of such high-altitude satellites in 1963 and 1964: the Syncom series. Millions of television viewers far from Asia were able to watch live TV coverage of the 1964 Tokyo Olympics thanks to the relays transmitted by Syncom 3.

The experience gained with these satellites led to the founding of the Communications Satellite Corporation, or "Comsat," a company designed to specialize entirely in space-relayed communications programs. Comsat orbited its initial satellite, Early Bird, in 1965. It was capable of providing 240 telephone circuits or one TV channel between North America and Europe. When it was joined in 1967 by two companions—Intelsat 2 over the Pacific and Intelsat 3 over the Atlantic—all the world's TV networks could be linked together. The first global telecast took place on June 27, 1967. Today, relays of live telecasts originating in almost any part of the world have become everyday affairs, and viewers in the United States can watch the funeral of a French President, the fighting in an African civil war, or the visit of a Pope to Australia while the actual events are occurring.

Communications satellites are just beginning to affect our lives. Before long, they may change our world beyond recognition, and alter the patterns of business and society at least as much as the telephone has done. They may give us instant "newspapers," with updated hourly editions flashed onto portable receivers no bigger than this book; they may make all telephone calls local ones, so that it will be just as quick and cheap to call a friend in South America or the Near East as one next door; they may lead to the development of worldwide styles of dress and living habits, and even a single worldwide language. Whether we like it or not, the world of the communications satellites will be one world (Plate 17).

If political tensions remain, however, space satellites will also continue to serve as super-spies, as they have done since the earliest years of the space age. Military reconnaissance satellites, flying in the no-man's-land beyond the atmosphere, take pictures of anything and everything. The United States and the Soviet Union have each launched whole platoons of them to keep watch over the movements of troops, to search for hidden missile sites, to survey what navies and air forces are doing. Some of these space vehicles are mere eyes in the sky, relaying thousands of photographs; others listen in to radar and communications networks. Some are equipped to detect unauthorized nuclear explosions; some are involved in precision mapping and navigation.

The uses of space satellites, then, seem almost infinite. Scarcely a week goes by now without a new one joining the multitude of orbiting objects already aloft. From some we derive obscure and specialized data that can be understood and appreciated only by scientists. Other satellites serve our national security. And others are no further from our daily lives than our telephones and television sets.

7

Stations in Space

We here in the late twentieth century, looking up at the ocean of space, can hardly begin to guess at the things that men may be doing out there when the year 2000 arrives. But we can be fairly sure that there will be many scientists floating on permanent orbiting space stations a few thousand miles above the Earth, studying not only the stars around them but also the planet looming beneath.

Valuable as the reports from unmanned satellites have been, a manned space station would be immensely more useful. A good example is provided by weather satellites. Though these have sent enormous amounts of data to Earth, this is only a tiny fraction of that available even to the naked human eye; the best TV pictures simply cannot equal what the eye alone can take in. Also, the robot automatic systems are unselective and often transmit virtually the same information over and over again. A human observer, especially one who was a trained meteorologist, could concentrate on areas of particular interest, focus special instruments on them, and ignore those that were not important (Plate 14). Although in theory this sort of thing could be done with robot systems, there comes a point when it is cheaper and more effective to have the decision-making computer (that is, a human being) right on the spot.

Manned laboratories in space hold new possibilities for physics and astronomy, too. What has been accomplished by the present scientific satellites could be multiplied many times over if scientists were directly guiding the research equipment from space. Anyone who thinks otherwise may try to imagine how fast science would have progressed if all experiments and observations had to be carried out via remote-controlled handling devices and TV screens. Even the simplest piece of scientific equipment requires innumerable adjustments, and this is particularly true of new and untried apparatus designed to extend the frontiers of knowledge.

Space stations may also one day be used as hospitals and for medical research. Their advantages for this purpose stem from the weightless condition that would exist in them. Many kinds of muscular and heart disease could be treated much more readily when the patient's weakened body had much less work to do owing to the absence of weight. And anyone who has ever suffered from bedsores will know what a boon a low or zero gravity environment could be; and for serious burns, or therapy following an operation, it might make the difference between life and death.

These are only some of the possible uses of space stations. When space travel is as fully established as air transport is today, some of these stations may become veritable spaceports, where interplanetary liners and short-range ferry rockets from Earth meet to exchange

passengers and cargo. There seems no limit to the ultimate possibilities, and perhaps one day there may be
millions of people living in space-cities and looking down
with scorn upon the inhabitants of Earth exhausting themselves, and perhaps shortening their lives, in their endless struggle against gravity.

How might such stations in space be built, and what
would they look like (Plates 10 and 11)? Clearly, they
could not be constructed on Earth and carried up in any
rocket, however big. That might be suitable for the early
experimental three- or five-man stations like the United
States' "sky lab," but the ambitious ones of the day after
tomorrow will have to be assembled in space from pre-
fabricated parts.

Suppose it were decided to set up a space station at
a height of 4,000 miles. To stay in its orbit, the station
would have to move at about 12,000 miles an hour, and
would take four hours to complete one circuit around
the Earth. Its parts—designed to be small enough to fit
in the cargo hold of a freight-carrying rocket—would
be boosted to the desired orbit. Then the hatches would
be opened, and the cargo would be quite literally dumped
in space. A low-powered radio beacon would probably
be attached to it so that it could be found without
difficulty on later trips.

When the freighter returned to Earth for its next load, it
would leave behind a miscellaneous collection of boxes
and girders, tied together with ropes to prevent them
from drifting apart. They would go on revolving round the
world with clockwork precision, so that astronomers could
tell within a few miles where they would be a thousand

years later. There would be no danger of anything happening to them; in the airlessness of space, girders would not rust.

Eventually, after many trips by the freighter rockets, all the bits and pieces would have been gathered together in orbit. Then the construction crews would start work. Wearing spacesuits, they would be operating under some difficulties, but they would also have several great advantages. Most important of all, nothing would have any weight. The largest girder, given a gentle push, would start to move slowly *and would continue to move* until brought to rest again. Much of the work of assembly could be done by hauling on ropes, but a good deal of the time the workmen would have to use small propulsive devices for moving around—like the gas-powered "maneuvering gun" held by Edward White during his famous Gemini 4 spacewalk. A nozzle on a cylinder of compressed gas could be opened, thus acting as a sort of cold rocket, in moving from place to place; or pistols would shoot them about through the force of their recoil.

The complete absence of "up" or "down" would at first be very confusing, but the human brain is highly adaptable and the workmen would soon come to take their "space acrobatics" for granted. They would be reassured, also, by the fact that they could step back and look at their work with no danger of falling—which they certainly could not do if they were building skyscrapers back on Earth!

A great many designs for space stations have been put forward by students of the subject, but most of them have several features in common. First of all, of course, the station must be airtight so that the men inside it don't have to wear spacesuits all the time. Its temperature must also be controlled, and, in fact, it would have to have all the gadgets necessary on a spaceship apart from the rocket motors themselves. Indeed, it might even be fitted with very low-powered rockets, so that it could make minor adjustments to its orbit when necessary.

Most designers of space stations have proposed the use of large mirrors to collect sunlight and thus provide power. Out in space, in direct sunlight, almost two horsepower of heat energy fall on every square yard—and when you realize how far away from the Sun we are, that gives you some faint idea of its total energy. Two horsepower per square yard over the entire surface of a sphere 93,000,000 miles in radius (that is, a sphere embracing the Earth's orbit) is an impressive figure! It seems a pity to waste this energy, and it could easily be collected by suitable mirrors and used to run some kind of turbine, thus producing the electricity needed in the station.

Another popular idea is to have the space stations disk-shaped or wheel-shaped, and slowly revolving. By this means, it would be possible to have a kind of artificial gravity inside, because centrifugal force would come into play. The people inside the station would be pressed against the rim of the wheel, and the resulting sensation of weight would be exactly like the real thing. The effect would get smaller as one went toward the center, and at the middle of the wheel there would be no "weight" at all.

The spin would be quite slow, as only a small amount of artificial gravity would be needed, just enough to enable one to walk around in the normal way, and to keep objects from drifting about in the air as they would if there were no weight at all (Figure 3). A wheel 600 feet in diameter—about the size of the "Hilton Orbiter" shown in *2001: A Space Odyssey*—would have to turn three times a minute to produce a force equal to normal earth weight at its rim.

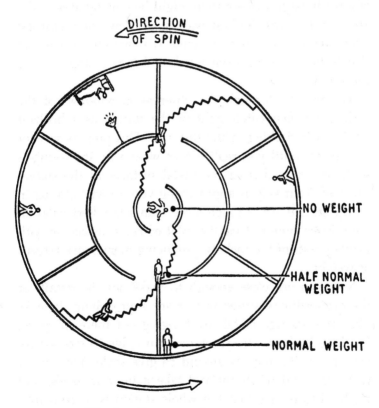

Fig. 3. Gravity in the space-station.

The space station would be set spinning in the first place by attaching small rockets to its rim and firing them for a calculated period of time. After that it would keep on revolving forever, just as the Earth does, because there would be no friction to slow it down.

This spin would, however, introduce complications when one tried to get aboard the station: it would be rather like climbing on a merry-go-round in full swing, for the rim of a really large space station might be moving at 60 miles an hour. Perhaps the best way to see how one might get over this difficulty is to imagine that we are in a rocket that has climbed up from Earth and is now approaching the station.

As you look through the observation windows of the rocket, you first catch sight of the station as a brilliant light slowly flashing in the distance. This puzzles you for a moment, until you realize that what you are seeing is sunlight reflected from the metal surfaces as the station revolves. Your ship is approaching very slowly, closing in on the station at not much more than a hundred miles an hour. From time to time the pilot corrects his course with gentle bursts of the rockets, producing momentary returns of weight.

Now you are close enough to make out the details of the extraordinary structure you are approaching. It looks like some strange metal toy hanging out there in space, for there is no way in which you can judge its size—there are no familiar objects around to give scale. You almost feel you could reach out and take it in your hands, and it's hard to realize that the whole station is more than a hundred feet across.

Not until you are less than a mile away, and can see such details as observation windows and radio aerials, can you really judge its true size. It's shaped like a giant cartwheel with four spokes, and the resemblance is increased by the presence of an axle at the center. Using mere fizzles from his steering jets, the pilot is cautiously making his way toward this axle.

That's funny—the space-station is revolving, but the axle isn't! Now you understand how you are going to go aboard. The axis of the station is really a hollow tube, not rigidly fixed to the station which is thus "freewheeling" around it. So it's safe for your spaceship and the axle to be connected together.

There's a soft thump as contact is made, inflated bumpers taking up the shock of impact. Men in spacesuits have emerged from the station and are connecting cables to your ship. Presently there are various clangings and scratchings from the airlock, and a steady hissing (which is highly disconcerting at first!) as pressure equalizes. Then the airlock doors open, and you're free to go into the station.

You're still weightless, of course, as you float through the hollow tube, and at its end you emerge into a big drum-shaped chamber. It's very slowly turning around you, and men appear to be standing on the walls, looking up at you. There are some hand-holds conveniently placed where you can grip them as they move slowly past, and with the slightest of jerks you take up the spin of the station. It's really no more difficult than stepping onto a moving escalator (Figure 4). As you start to move you feel weight again. At first it's very slight, perhaps not more than ten pounds, but it will increase as you go out-ward toward the more rapidly moving rim of the station.

Not all space stations may be given spin, for in some cases it might be desirable to be completely weightless. The astronomers, with their big telescopes, would also find it highly inconvenient if their observatories turned completely around every ten seconds or so. In cases like these, two stations might be built within a few miles of each other. One would be the living quarters, and would be spinning so that, when they were sleeping or off duty, the scientists would have normal weight. The other—the space laboratory—would have no spin, and the staff would move across from one to the other in small, very low-powered rocket ferries or shuttles.

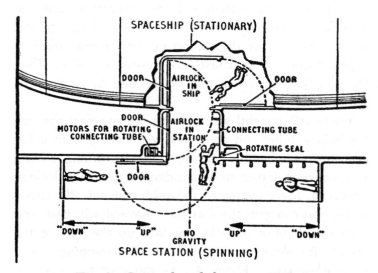

Fig. 4.   Going aboard the space-station.

These shuttles would play much the same sort of role in space as the familiar jeep has done here on Earth. Indeed, one can well imagine that they would be christened "space jeeps"! Their job would be to move objects around outside the space stations, or to make trips from one station to another. They would have no streamlining, of course, and would probably be little more than stubby cylinders with a small rocket motor at one end. A top speed of a few hundred miles an hour is all that they would need for most purposes, and because of their low power it might take them several minutes to reach this. They then could coast, if need be, for thousands of miles until they came to their destination and had to use their rockets again to make a safe approach.

There is certainly something about the space station, floating forever high above the world, that catches the imagination almost as much as the idea of traveling to other planets. The first stations will be very small and very close, perhaps circling only five hundred miles up and carrying half a dozen men in very cramped conditions. It may be fifty years or more before the ambitious space cities we have talked about are finally built. They would be easily visible to the naked eye, as are some of the larger unmanned satellites already launched. At night one might see them as tiny, swiftly moving stars; under favorable conditions, they could even be seen in the daytime. And they would have one very peculiar characteristic. The closer stations would rise in the west and go backward across the sky, setting in the *east*—the exact opposite of all the other heavenly bodies!

A little thought will show why this would happen. We

see the stars rise in the east because the Earth is turning toward that direction once every 24 hours. But a space station would move around the world in a few hours—perhaps in as little as 90 minutes—much more quickly, therefore, than the Earth itself turns on its axis. It would thus overtake Earth's rotation and climb up out of the *western* sky.

There's a common example of this sort of thing that everyone has seen. When you are in a train moving at 30 miles an hour and an express passes you at a much greater speed, you seem to be moving backward. This is an example of what is called relative velocity.

We have seen that, once a station has been given the correct speed for its particular orbit, it could never fall down but would carry on, circling the Earth forever. The only danger that could seriously threaten it would be meteors, and since these seem to scare a lot of people, let's see how much of a menace they really represent.

First of all, what exactly is a meteor? Well, it's a fragment of rock or metal traveling through space—perhaps part of the general debris left over when the planets were formed. The total number of meteors in the whole of space is inconceivably huge, for billions of them come into our atmosphere every day. The vast majority are burned up by friction in the atmosphere, and only a very few of the larger ones reach the ground. Every so often meteors weighing several pounds, or even tons, fall to Earth, but these are so rare that in all history there are only a couple of cases of men having been killed by them.

Above the protecting shield of the atmosphere, however, one might expect to encounter meteors of every size.

and even the tiny ones might be dangerous because of their tremendous speeds—up to 150,000 miles an hour. At such velocities, a meteor the size of a pinhead could do more damage than a rifle bullet. Before the Space Age, this made some people jump to the conclusion that spaceships would be promptly riddled as soon as they got beyond the atmosphere.

Fortunately, although there are so many meteors, there is a lot more of space, and, when you work out the chances of being hit by anything large enough to do damage, you find that spaceships on reasonably short journeys have nothing to worry about. This was demonstrated by the three huge Pegasus satellites launched by the United States in 1965. Once in orbit, these satellites unfolded vast "wings," almost a hundred feet across, made of thin aluminum panels wired so as to register all meteor impacts and transmit the information to Earth. After many months of successful operation, the three Pegasus satellites showed that the chances of a meteor collision in space are actually quite slender. During the course of a few years, however, a space station might expect some punctures unless it took suitable precautions. A great deal of protection could be obtained by the simple device of giving the station a double wall, which would probably be done in any case for other reasons.

Once in many years, both walls would be penetrated, but even this need not be serious. True, the air would start to rush out, but it would take several minutes before the pressure dropped to a dangerously low value, and there would be plenty of time to seal the leak.

There may be other dangers and problems which will

have to be overcome before we can build space stations—
such as radiation in space. The Van Allen belt has turned
out to be less of a hazard than originally feared, but the
colossal eruptions on the face of the Sun known as solar
flares may spray immense areas of space with possibly
lethal particles. This is not certain, though; and unknown
dangers often have a habit of disappearing when they are
firmly faced, like the imaginary sea monsters that Colum-
bus was undoubtedly warned against when he set sail
toward the west.

8

The Heavens Around Us

The time has now come for us to look farther into space—
far beyond the remotest of the satellite space stations we
discussed in the last chapter. We're going to make a
quick tour of the universe, to discover something about
the places we will be visiting as the coming phases of the
space age unfold.

When you look up at the sky on a clear night, it seems
packed with stars. It is hard to believe—and it was many
thousands of years before it was discovered—that all
those stars are suns. Most of those that you can see are
at least as bright as our own Sun, and some of them are
hundreds or thousands of times brighter. Yet they are at
such great distances that they appear merely as points
of light, giving no trace of heat. Almost all are at least
a *million* times farther away than our Sun—or, to put it
in another way, if our Sun were carried off to a million
times its present distance, it would be just another star,
and a faint one at that.

If all the stars were suddenly wiped out of existence,
it would make no difference at all to us here on Earth—
they are so very far away. Let's imagine that this improb-
able catastrophe has happened, and consider what would
be left.

First of all, of course, there would be the Sun and the

Moon. They look almost exactly the same size, but, as was long ago discovered, the Sun is really much bigger and much farther away. Without its heat, life on Earth would be impossible, and it is for us, therefore, by far the most important body in the sky. Its enormous gravity field keeps the Earth and planets moving regularly in their orbits. There is, of course, no question of our ever going to the Sun itself, because it is so hot that no metal could remain solid, or even liquid, at its surface. Moreover, its gravity is so great that you would weigh 28 times as much there as you would on Earth, and that alone would be enough to kill you instantly.

Conditions are very different on the Moon, which is a much smaller world than ours and only 240,000 miles away, as compared with the 93,000,000 miles to the Sun. Nevertheless, the total area of the Moon is as much as that of the whole continent of Africa, so it will take us quite a while to explore it all. The Moon, like the Earth and all the other planets, has no light of its own and shines only by the reflected glory of the Sun.

Even if we abolished the stars, the Sun and Moon would not be the only objects left in the suddenly emptied skies. There would be five other brilliant lights, looking just like stars but moving in the heavens in a way the stars never did. These would be the planets, and you would seldom see more than two or three of them in the sky at any one time.

Two of the most brilliant of the planets keep close to the Sun, and so you may see them in the morning or the evening, but never in the midnight sky. This is because they travel around the Sun well *inside* the orbit of Earth. Even amid the glare of cities, people sometimes look up and see, in the early evening when the Sun has just set, the dazzlingly brilliant glare of Venus, hanging like a tiny arc lamp in the sky. It is so brilliant, indeed, that it is quite easy to see in broad daylight if you know exactly where to look.

The other planet inside Earth's orbit is Mercury, so close to the Sun that it is not often noticed, though it is quite a brilliant object when you can catch it against the sunset glow.

Since they all move around the Sun in roughly circular paths, with the Sun at the center, the distances between the planets are continually altering. At its nearest, Venus is 26,000,000 miles away from Earth and thus comes closer to us than any other planet. Unfortunately, we can't see much of it on these occasions, as it is then between us and the Sun. That means not only that it is lost in the Sun's glare, but also that its dark side is turned toward us.

Besides Venus and Mercury, there would be three other bright planets visible from time to time. You would often be able to see them high in the southern sky at midnight— in other words, as far away from the Sun as they could possibly get. A little thought shows that this means they must move on paths *outside* the Earth's orbit, unlike Mercury and Venus, so that we are able to get between them and the Sun.

These three planets are Mars, Jupiter, and Saturn. At their closest to us they are, respectively, 35,000,000 miles, 390,000,000 miles, and 793,000,000 miles away. You will see from these last figures that the inner planets, Mercury, Venus, and Earth, are quite crowded together compared with the outer ones.

This list contains all the planets that were known to us before the invention of the telescope. Together with the Sun and Moon, they would be the only visible objects left in the sky if the stars suddenly disappeared. There are, however, three more planets—Uranus, Neptune, and Pluto—which you would need a telescope to see. They are all farther away than Saturn, and the last one of all, Pluto, is 3,675,000,000 miles from the Sun. It is quite likely that there are still other planets beyond Pluto, but at such great distances they would be almost impossible to see from Earth with presently available means. So at the moment Pluto represents the frontier of the Sun's domain.

Picture, then, this little family of worlds, all revolving in the same direction around their giant central Sun. Our own Earth is the third from the center, and it's not a very conspicuous member of the family. True, four of the planets—Mercury, Venus, Mars, and Pluto—are smaller than Earth. However, the other four—Jupiter, Saturn, Uranus, and Neptune—are *very* much bigger.

One of the lessons that astronomy teaches us is that there is nothing very outstanding or unusual about our place in the universe. We've no reason to be ashamed of our planet, but no reason to boast about it either!

Most of the planets have satellites, or moons, revolving round them. Our world, of course, has one, which we call *the* Moon. Mars has two, Jupiter twelve, Saturn ten, Uranus five, Neptune two. Mercury and Venus have none, and Pluto is too far away for us to tell. Most of these moons are very small indeed (though two of Jupiter's and one of Saturn's are larger than the planet Mercury) and there are probably many others that we have not yet discovered.

All the planets, except perhaps Mercury, have atmospheres—that is, they are surrounded by layers of gas. Some of these layers are enormously thick and dense; others—like that of Mars—very thin indeed. Unfortunately, there is not a single other planet with an atmosphere which we could breathe, so anything you may have read about people like us living on the neighboring worlds is simply not true. In Chapter 12 we'll have a closer look at conditions on the planets, but we can say right away that there's no other place like Earth, at least not in this corner of the universe. This means, of course, that any forms of life we may meet on the other eight planets will be quite strange. That makes the prospect of interplanetary travel all the more exciting. How dull things would be if each planet were just like the rest!

Although the distances between the planets seem so enormous by our usual standards, that is not as great a handicap to space flight as one might think. Between the worlds there is a perfect vacuum, and hence no air resistance at all. Thus a spaceship would not lose any of its original velocity through friction, and under the proper conditions could keep up its speed forever, just as the Earth does in its eternal circling of the Sun. So interplanetary flight is largely a question of aiming yourself in the right direction, building up the necessary speed— and then sitting back to wait.

The Sun and its family of planets form what is known as the solar system, and despite its size this system is a very tiny affair when compared with the distances to the other suns—the stars. For example, the *very nearest* star is almost 10,000 times as far away as the remotest planet, Pluto. This means that when we have explored all the planets we will be nowhere near conquering the enormously greater distances to the stars.

However, the eight planets and 32 moons should keep us busy for some centuries to come—and at the end of that time, no doubt, men will be speculating about the possibility of inter*stellar* travel in just the same way as we speculate about inter*planetary* travel today.

For the closest of our heavenly neighbors, of course, such travel is no longer a matter of speculation. Explorers from Earth have already reached the Moon, just a short hop away. (Venus, nearest of the planets, is more than a hundred times further from us.) Although voyages to the Moon are not yet everyday affairs, many of you who are reading these words will live to see an era in which spaceships take off for it with monotonous regularity. And some of you, it is safe to say, will make the journey yourselves, setting foot on the same barren landscape that so far has been invaded only by a handful of astronauts. Let's follow you now on one of those voyages—those great adventures of the future. . . .

9

Flight to the Moon

It's four minutes to blastoff, and you're trying to tell yourself that you aren't *really* afraid. The pilot has finished checking his instruments, and from time to time a voice from the control tower comes through a loudspeaker. Otherwise it is quiet—almost too quiet. To occupy your mind, you examine the masses of instruments and try to decide what they all do. Some of them, the fuel, pressure, and temperature gauges, for example, are obvious, but there are others of which you can't make head or tail. You wonder how anyone can ever learn what they're all for.

Suddenly an electric motor starts to whir close at hand. Then things begin to happen all over the place: switches click, powerful pumps begin to whine, valves start to snap open down in the heart of the great rocket in whose streamlined nose you are sitting. With each new noise you think, "This is it!"—but still you don't move. When the voyage finally begins, you aren't prepared for it.

A long way off, it seems, there's a noise like a thousand waterfalls, or a thunderstorm in which the crashes follow each other so quickly that there's no moment of silence between them. The rocket motors have started, but are not yet delivering enough power to lift the ship. Quickly the roar mounts, the cabin begins to vibrate, and the spaceship rises. Outside, the launching pad is being sprayed with flame for a hundred yards around.

Something seems to be pushing you down, quite gently, into the thick cushion of your couch. It isn't at all uncomfortable, but the pressure mounts until your limbs seem to be made of lead and it takes a deliberate effort to keep breathing. You try to lift your hand, and the labor needed to move it even a few inches is so tiring that you let it drop back beside you. You lie limp and relaxed, waiting to see what will happen next. You're no longer frightened. It's too exciting for that, this feeling of infinite power sweeping you up into the sky.

There's a sudden fall in the thunder of the rockets, the sensation of immense weight ebbs away and you can breathe more easily. Power is being reduced; in a few moments, Earth will no longer be able to recapture you. A minute later silence comes flooding back as the motors cut out completely, and all feeling of weight vanishes. For a few minutes the pilot checks his instruments; then he turns around and smiles.

"Nicely on course; we'll make our rendezvous in forty minutes. You can get up if you want to."

Gingerly you ease yourself out of the couch, holding onto it with one hand. You feel rather like a captive balloon as you float there in space; then you pluck up courage and gently push yourself across the cabin. You float slowly over to the observation port, anxious to have a look at Earth.

What you see, however, is so wonderful that it takes your breath away. Almost filling the sky is a tremendous, blinding crescent, the shape of a new moon but hundreds of times bigger. The rocket is passing over the night side of Earth, and most of the planet is in darkness. You can see it dimly as a vast, shadowy circle eclipsing the stars. Here and there are patches of brightness—the lights of great cities.

As you wait, the narrow crescent slowly grows and presently you are looking down on the sunlit side of the planet. It's taken you just over 40 minutes to travel half-way around the world! Then the pilot tells you to go back to your couch while he "homes in" on the spaceship that's already circling up here, waiting for you to go aboard.

It's an ugly-looking machine, nothing like the sleek, streamlined torpedo of a booster that carried you up from Earth. In fact, it's a stubby cylinder, rounded at one end and with a shock-absorbing undercarriage at the other. The rounded end is fitted with several windows and a lot of radio equipment, while between the undercarriage legs you can see the jets of rocket nozzles.

This is the Lunar Shuttle, which spends all its time in space. Its job is to circle the Earth and pick up passengers and supplies bound for the colony on the Moon. Moving in its orbit above the atmosphere at 18,000 miles an hour, it needs no great output of energy to build up the extra 7,000 mph that will let it escape from the Earth. Its rocket motors are far too weak to enable it to land on Earth or take off again, but they are powerful enough to fight the Moon's much weaker gravity, so that the Shuttle can make the trip down to the Moon and back again to its orbit around Earth.

It's several hours later, and you're now aboard the Shuttle waiting for the *real* journey to begin. The rocket that carried you up from Earth has been flown back to its launching pad; the days when a rocket was discarded after a single mission are long since over. The first lap of your journey is finished; climbing that hundred miles has taken more fuel than is needed for the quarter of a million miles that remain.

The Shuttle is quite large, and a couple of passengers are already aboard. They came up, you gather, on an earlier ferry flight. They welcome you and the others who have come on your flight. Since the journey is going to last several days, there are little bunks in which you can sleep, and there's a tiny lounge in which you can sit and read or look at the stars.

At last everything is ready. The pilot waits for the carefully calculated instant and starts the motors. This time, the force urging you down into your couch is very gentle—hardly enough, in fact, to give you your normal weight. The Shuttle is taking its time to build up speed, to add the extra 7,000 mph that will tear it away from Earth. The vibration of the rockets lasts for many minutes; then silence falls and your weight vanishes once more. It will not return until you reach the Moon.

Yet everything still seems exactly the same. The Earth hasn't moved, and you still appear to be going around it just as before. You'll have to wait awhile if you want to see any change.

An hour later there's no doubt about it. Earth is a good deal smaller; it's slowly falling astern. You're traveling outward on the long curve which, without any more effort on the part of the rockets, will take you to the Moon. . . (Figure 5).

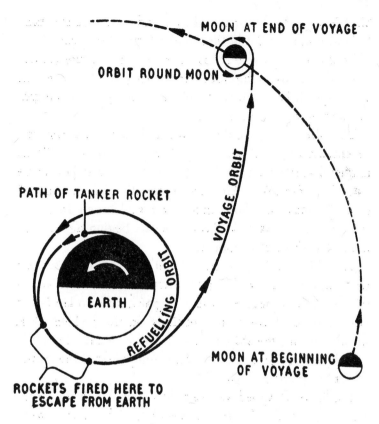

Fig. 5.   The Earth-Moon trip.

Space travel may sound exciting, but in fact you're
rather bored before the two days of the journey are up.
All that happens is that Earth slowly shrinks astern, while
the Moon slowly grows ahead. Since there is no sensation
of motion whatsoever, only logic tells you that you're really
approaching the Moon. The nose of the ship isn't pointing
anywhere in particular; in fact, as it travels along, the

Shuttle very slowly turns end over end. Not until it is time to land will the pilot bother to check the ship's spin.

That time has come at last. For some hours, the gravity field of the Moon has been increasing—and so has the ship's speed. But you can't feel this, since you are weightless as the ship is in free fall.

The Moon is now only a few hundred miles away, and so enormous that it seems to fill the sky. Indeed, it's no longer a globe hanging in space but a jagged landscape spread out far below. You can see countless mountains and craters, many of whose names you've learned from the maps in the past few days. They're beginning to look much too close for comfort. . . .

The ship is falling at over 5,000 miles an hour toward that inhospitable world. Since there is no trace of an atmosphere, you can't use wings or parachutes to land, and will therefore have to rely entirely on the rockets. That means turning the ship around in space so that the jets—and the elaborate shock-absorbing equipment of the undercarriage—point downward.

You have strapped yourself into your couch when the pilot begins the landing maneuvers. The stars sweep around you as the ship turns in space. Nothing has happened to its speed yet, but the low-powered steering jets have swung the Shuttle around into the right position for landing. The pilot is watching his instruments intently —but he is not touching the controls, for the final landing is quite automatic. It is controlled by a computer aboard ship, which uses radar to measure the distance to the ground. The human pilot merely stands by in case something goes wrong—in which case he would use his judgment to try to make an emergency landing or to climb out into space again.

With a roar that seems doubly impressive after the long hours of silence, the motors thunder into life. There's a sudden feeling of returning weight, and through the observation window you can just glimpse the white-hot pillar of flame that's checking your headlong fall against the Moon, still many miles below. The spaceship is dropping toward the heart of a great ring of mountains. Presently, when the roar of the rocket ceases, some of the taller peaks already seem to be towering above the ship. For a few seconds you are falling free once more, and for a horrible moment you wonder if power has failed and you are about to crash on those cruel hills. Then the rockets flare out again, and the scene below vanishes in fire and clouds of dust blasted up by the jet. A moment later there's the gentlest of impacts, then utter silence.

You are on the Moon.

10

The Moon

Although the Moon may seem small and unimportant compared with the planets, its nearness makes up for this, and the first great extraterrestrial explorations have taken place on its desolate landscape. Even before man sent his first vehicles into space we had very good maps of its surface. Tens of thousands of craters were carefully charted, and more than a thousand of them were given names, mostly after great philosophers or scientists.

Observation by means of telescopes not only gave us a good idea of the Moon's geography, but allowed us to determine what it was actually like there. The fact that no clouds could be seen on the Moon proved that it has no atmosphere, and therefore no life of the type that exists on Earth. And with our modern instruments we were able to learn, at a distance of 240,000 miles, such facts as the temperature of the lunar surface—more than 200°F at noon, less than −200°F at night.

Reconnaissance flights by unmanned space probes told us much more (Plates 18 and 19). Several Russian and American probes reached the vicinity of the Moon as early as 1959; the Soviet Luna 2 made history's first landing there on September 13 of that year—and in October, 1959, Luna 3 sent back photographs taken from orbit around the Moon. These revealed something that had been hidden from the

human race since the beginning of history—the far side of
the Moon, which is always turned away from Earth.

Technical difficulties caused a gap of nearly five years
before the next useful flight to the Moon. America's unmanned Ranger 7 probe, carrying six TV cameras, crash-
landed on the lunar surface in July, 1964, transmitting
4,316 pictures during the last 15 minutes of its flight. The
final one, taken 1,000 feet above the surface of the Moon,
showed little craters only a few feet in diameter. Until
then the best telescopes had been unable to detect objects
less than half a mile across. Several other Ranger probes
followed, and then, in January, 1966, the Russian Luna 9
achieved the first "soft"—that is, noncrash—landing on
the Moon. After its gentle descent this probe relayed data
that proved that the Moon's crust was strong enough to
support the weight of a spaceship. Previously, some scientists had argued that the Moon might be covered by a
deep, soft layer of dust, and that our first spacecraft, at-
tempting to land there, would sink gently into this dust
and never be seen again.

The Surveyor probes that the United States planted on
the Moon in 1966 and 1967 increased our knowledge of
what future astronauts might expect (Plate 21). Surveyor 3
carried a mechanical claw with which it scratched trenches
in the ground around it. It found a layer of unmistakable
soil, as thick as damp sand (although it was not damp!), and
one space scientist commented, "The soil behaves in a dis-
appointingly ordinary way." Pioneering moonwalker Neil
Armstrong of Apollo XI reported as he took his first steps,
"The surface is fine and powdery. I can pick it up loosely
with my toe. . . . I only go in a small fraction of an inch,

maybe an eighth of an inch. But I can see the footprints of my boots and the treads in the fine sandy particles."

When several expeditions have landed safely on the Moon, carried out wide-ranging explorations, and returned to Earth, the next step will be to set up a permanent scientific base there. It will probably be largely underground to avoid the great variation in temperature between the lunar day and night, which last almost 30 times as long as ours. (At the surface, as we've seen, there's a difference of more than 400° F. between noon and midnight. However, a few feet down the temperature hardly varies day or night.)

In many ways, the Moon will be an even better site for an astronomical observatory than a space station would be. Visibility will be just as good, and there will be firm anchorage for the largest instruments. The fact that the Moon turns so slowly on its axis—once in 27 *days* as compared with Earth's once in 24 *hours*—will also be a considerable advantage to the astronomers. Even during the lunar day it would be easy to observe the stars, because there is no atmosphere to scatter the sunlight and to swamp the stars in its glare. With a properly shielded telescope, one could observe the stars right up to the edge of the Sun.

The Moon will provide plenty of work for scientists of all sorts. We have never had a chance of examining any world except our own, and almost every branch of science will make great advances when we can carry out experiments and make investigations in a totally strange environment. Geologists are already at work trying to discover the origin of the thousands of craters and circular "walled plains" that cover so much of the Moon's surface

(Plates 12 and 15). Were they caused, as some scientists think, by the impact of enormous meteors? If so, why are some areas almost free of them? Or were they, on the other hand, entirely "home-grown"—produced by volcanic forces inside the Moon itself? Results so far indicate that both views may be right. The biggest of these lunar features seem almost certainly to be the result of immense impacts, but there is also ample evidence of volcanic activity.

The first lunar base will have to be supplied from Earth, in much the same way as research stations in the Antarctic are provisioned from home. However, because the cost of transport will be so great, it will be necessary to make the base self-supporting at the earliest possible moment.

Since there is no air or water, this idea may seem fantastic, but it's really nothing of the sort. For what is air? The important part is the oxygen, and oxygen is one of the main constituents of most rocks. It makes up no less than *half* the crust of the Earth, and the proportion is almost the same on the Moon. Because it will be combined chemically, it will require heat and other means to set it free; but atomic power should provide all the energy we need for this sort of operation. Eventually, therefore, the lunar colony will be able to build up its own stocks of the precious gas and will have no need to import any from Earth.

Water must also be present on the Moon, as it is on Earth, combined with various salts and other chemicals in many types of rock. When we have had a chance to do some extensive lunar prospecting, we should be able to locate supplies of any material we need. It would then be possible to grow crops on the Moon in pressurized greenhouses, feeding the growing plants on chemicals produced from the Moon itself. The method of cultivation known as hydroponic or soilless farming would be very suitable for this purpose. In this system, the plants are supported on wire netting and their roots dip into solutions of the necessary salts. Crops can be grown far more rapidly than under normal conditions, and also take up much less space. The fourteen days of continuous sunlight which one would have during the lunar "day" would also make things much easier for the farmer!

Altogether apart from purely scientific reasons, there are extremely powerful practical incentives for the colonization of the Moon. Because of its low gravity, it is more than twenty times easier to escape from the Moon than from the Earth. If we can find sources of rocket propellants there, and thus set up refueling stations on the Moon, the problem of interplanetary flight will be enormously simplified.

Let's jump perhaps thirty years into the future, to a time when the Moon is no longer the frontier but has been fairly widely explored and settled. You're with a party of other colonists, leaving one of the underground bases on a trip across the surface. Surprisingly enough, you're making the journey in a very old-fashioned form of transport— a bus!

Old-fashioned or not, it's the only reasonable method. Rockets are far too expensive for short distances, and, since there is no atmosphere, normal air transport is out of the question. However, it's not at all an ordinary bus. It's airtight, of course, and is really a sort of mobile hotel in which a dozen people can live comfortably for a week.

The whole vehicle is about 40 feet long and is mounted on two sets of balloon tires with very deep treads; it is operated by powerful electric motors. The driver has a little raised cabin at the front, and the passenger compartment is fitted with comfortable seats that become bunks to sleep on. At the back is a kitchen, storeroom, and even a tiny shower stall.

The outer doors of the giant airlock leading into the underground garage have now opened, and you slowly climb up the ramp to the surface. Soon you're rolling briskly across the crater floor at about 40 miles an hour. It's easy to make good speed here as the ground is quite level and any obstacles have already been bulldozed out of the way to form the rough track you're following. You hope that there will soon be a change of scenery; it will be rather dull if it's like this all the way.

Before long your wish is granted. Far ahead, a line of sunlit peaks has become visible on the horizon, and minute by minute they climb higher in the sky. At first, because of the steep curvature of the Moon's surface, it seems that the bus is approaching nothing more than a modest range of hills, but presently you see that you're nearing a mountain wall several miles high. You look in vain for any pass or valley through which you can penetrate—and then, with a sick feeling in the pit of your stomach, you realize that your driver is making a frontal assault on that titanic barrier.

Ahead of you, the ground tilts abruptly in a slope as steep as the roof of a house. There's a sudden deepening in the vibration of the motors and then, scarcely checking its speed, the great bus charges up the endless, rock-strewn escarpment that seems to stretch ahead of you all the way to the stars.

Of course, there's no danger. This kind of straight-up driving would be impossible on Earth, but here, under a sixth of Earth's gravity, there's nothing to it.

Presently, when you've been climbing for many minutes, you look back across the great plain over which you've been traveling. As more and more of the crater wall comes into view, you see that it's built up in a series of vast terraces, the first of which you've just surmounted. In a few minutes you reach the crest, and turn along it instead of descending into the valley ahead. Far to the south, you can see the great crescent of Earth hanging low above the mountains. It's a blinding blue and white as its clouds and oceans reflect the sunlight back to you across a quarter of a million miles of space. When it is full, it will be far too bright to look at comfortably without tinted glasses.

It takes nearly two hours to reach the outer rim of the crater, two hours of doubling back and forth along great valleys, of exhilarating and terrifying charges up those impossible slopes. At last the whole of the walled plain lies spread out beneath you, and you can see once again the buildings of the colony, dwarfed by distance and with a tiny, toylike spaceship standing beside them.

You can travel more swiftly now, for the outer slopes are much less steep than those inside the crater, as is usually the case on the Moon. Even so, it's another two hours before you've finished the descent and are out in open country again.

One gets used to anything in time, even to driving across the Moon. The seasoned travelers have long ago settled down to conversations and games of cards, interrupted only when it is time for meals. At last, the featureless landscape now flowing uneventfully past lulls you to sleep. You operate the lever that turns your chair into a couch, and settle down for a nap.

You awake hours later, when the tilt of the bus tells you that you are climbing again. It's quite dark: the blinds have been drawn to keep out the sunlight still blazing from the black-velvet sky. Everyone is asleep; apart from the vibration and the tilt of the floor, you might be back on Earth in an airliner flying through the night. Presently the steady throb of the motors sends you to sleep once more.

The next time you wake the blinds are up, sunlight is shining into the cabin, and there's a pleasant smell of cooking from the little galley. The bus is moving rather slowly along the crest of a long range of hills, and you're surprised to see that all the other passengers are clustered around the observation window at the rear. Naturally, you go to join them.

You look back across the miles of land through which you have been traveling during your sleep. When you last saw it, Earth had been hanging low in the southern sky—but where is it now? Only the silver tip of its great crescent still shows above the horizon; while you've been sleeping, it's been dropping lower and lower in the sky.

You're passing over the rim of the Moon, into the mysterious, hidden land where the light of Earth never shines, the land that, before the coming of the rocket, no human eyes had ever seen.

Of course, the far side is mysterious no longer. It is as barren and as rugged and as forbidding as the side that faces Earth, although science fiction writers long ago had wistfully speculated it might be very different, even inhabited by living creatures. Though the first unmanned space probes to orbit the Moon proved that this was not so, the far side still somehow retains an air of romance— simply because no one *on* Earth can ever get a glimpse of it.

There's a simple reason for this odd state of affairs. Millions of years ago the Moon did revolve so that the whole of its surface could be seen from Earth. However, as it turned, great tides were raised in the Moon's partly pliable substance by our planet's attraction, and those tides acted in much the same way as the brake shoes on a wheel. Slowly, over the ages, they brought the Moon to rest, until now it remains with the same face turned always toward us.

The far side, incidentally, must never be called "the dark side," as is commonly done. It gets just as much sunlight as the side that looks toward Earth. But its long nights are lonely, for there is no brilliant Earth in the sky to illuminate the silent landscape. And as you go around the Moon's rim into that other hemisphere, you feel much farther away from home than you did a short time before, when you had only to look up into the sky to see the familiar continents of your own planet. . . .

11

To the Planets

When we start looking farther afield than the Moon and begin to consider the problem of reaching the planets, we make a surprising and encouraging discovery. Although the distances involved are often several hundred—or even thousand—times as great, interplanetary voyages require little more fuel than lunar ones. The reason for this is the fortunate fact, which we have already mentioned, that once you have built up any speed in space there is no resistance to destroy it again. If you simply sit back and wait, you will reach your destination in due course, assuming, naturally, that you have started off in the right direction!

There is one snag, though. Such journeys may not require much energy, but they consume a lot of time. The trip to the Moon takes less than five days—and only two or three if one starts with a little extra speed. However, the voyage to Venus, if you are trying to save fuel by taking the most economical path, lasts 145 days. The journey to Mars is even longer, about 260 days. It would certainly be boring to spend all that time in space, though it would probably be no worse than spending a winter snowed up in the Antarctic, as many polar explorers have done. A more serious objection is that such long journeys would use up a considerable amount of food and oxygen and thus make the supply problem difficult. And, of course, the longer one spends in space, the greater the chances of something going wrong—not to mention the dangers of meteors and cosmic rays.

It might be thought that it would be easiest to travel to the planets when they are at their nearest. Actually, just the opposite is true. This is because when the planets are closest to Earth they are moving past us—or we are moving past them—at very great speeds. For example, the speed of the Earth in its orbit around the Sun is 66,000 miles an hour; Venus moves a good deal faster, at 78,000 miles an hour. If we want to travel from Earth to Venus, therefore, we must somehow compensate for this difference of speed.

It turns out that the most economical way to do this is to let the spaceship fall in toward the Sun in such a way that it overtakes Venus, as shown in the diagram (Figure 6). When the spaceship leaves Earth, it fires its rockets for a few minutes to put it into the right orbit, and the Sun's gravity field does the rest. The ship becomes, in fact, a new planet for five months, and at the end of that time it will automatically arrive (if the original navigation was correct) at the orbit of Venus. The rockets then have to be fired for a few minutes to match the ship's speed to that of Venus, and then a landing can be made. The rockets might be firing for less than ten minutes on a journey that lasted 145 days! This is quite typical of the sort of thing that will happen in astronautics.

How is the pilot going to direct his ship accurately across so many millions of miles of space? Fortunately, this is a question which can already be answered in some

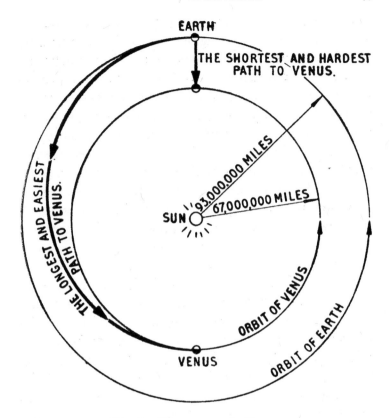

Fig. 6. The voyage to Venus.

detail. The science of astrogation—navigation by the stars—has been highly developed here on Earth for use at sea. By observing the heavenly bodies with his sextant (which is simply an instrument for measuring the number of degrees they are above the horizon), the captain of a ship in mid-ocean can determine his position to within a mile.

The same methods have been used in space to send unmanned probes to our neighboring planets, and will be used by astronauts when manned planetary voyaging begins. The instruments employed in astrogation are somewhat more complicated than those used at sea—and so are the calculations. The navigator of the spaceship, however, will have one great advantage which the captain of an ocean liner groping through fog might well envy. He will always be able to observe all the stars and planets, for there will never be any clouds to obscure his view. What is more, he will be able to see the complete skyful of stars, something we can never do on our own world, where the ground beneath our feet cuts off half the sky.

We should remember that even if the pilot makes a small mistake during the initial pull-away from Earth, he will be able to correct it later. For the spaceship can be steered, and its velocity altered, by further use of the rockets at any time in the voyage. However, because it takes so much fuel to make a major change in direction, it is essential for the navigation to be as precise as possible. A really bad error at the start would mean that the ship might head off in a direction from which it could not get back to any planet on its existing fuel reserve. And that would be fatal, for there would be no hope of rescue except under very exceptional circumstances. The unfortunate crewmen would travel on through space until they ran out of food or oxygen. No doubt the navigator responsible for the error would be the first to go through the airlock in order to conserve supplies. . . .

It would be very important for spaceships, like airplanes, to be able to communicate with their base or their home planet. Many of the complicated navigational calculations will be carried out by giant electronic computers, and the results radioed to the pilots in space. Also, quite apart from the practical value of good communications, it would be essential from the point of view of morale for ships to keep in touch with their bases during the weeks or months of their journeys. The crews would need some relaxation, and no doubt one day special programs will be broadcast from Earth to keep its far-flung sons and daughters in touch with home.

Everyone knows now that radio mesages, and even telecasts, can be sent from the Moon to the Earth. But the Moon is just across the road, astronomically speaking. Can we keep in touch with spaceships not merely thousands but millions, perhaps hundreds of millions, of miles away? The answer, of course, is yes. The Pioneer V space probe launched by the United States in 1960 settled that by sending radio messages to Earth from a distance of 20,000,-000 miles. Since then, other unmanned space probes have transmitted signals more than 200,000,000 miles, right across the width of the Earth's orbit.

Because radio waves travel at a speed of 186,000 miles a second, there must always be a time-lag before one could get a reply from anybody in space. At the Moon's distance, the delay is quite small—less than three seconds. For Mars and Venus, however, the lag would be several minutes even when they were closest to Earth; and it would take more than *five hours* for a radio signal to make the journey from Pluto.

Today, when we have built only a few small three-man spaceships, it is obviously impossible to guess how large

or how swift they may ultimately become. But looking
back and seeing how vessels of sea and air have developed,
it seems safe to predict that the spaceships of a few centuries hence may carry very large numbers of people on
perfect safety between the planets. They will be powered
by atomic energy, perhaps, and may operate some kind of
electric rocket of the kind mentioned in Chapter 3. It is
even posible that some new principle of propulsion may
have been discovered, but that is pure guesswork. We
know that the rocket can do the job; it will be nice if
something better turns up, but if not we'll do without it.
Maybe the real spaceliners will spin slowly as they travel
through space, to give the passengers a sensation of
weight. This idea is attractive from some points of view,
and it may prove essential if prolonged periods of weightlessness have any dangerous effects. The longest space
voyages to date have lasted only a few weeks, and physi-
cians suspect that a journey of many months under weightless conditions may harm the body. However, spinning the
ship would introduce complications of its own. One can
well imagine the passengers developing bad cases of space
sickness as they watch the stars revolving completely
around the sky every few seconds!

The first interplanetary spaceships, as we have seen,
will need several months to make the journeys even to
such nearby worlds as Mars and Venus. But, as for all
other forms of transport, speeds will steadily increase. The
long, lonely months of the first pioneers will be carved
down to weeks, and eventually to days. There is no limit
to speed in space, at least—according to Einstein's theory
of relativity—not until one begins to approach the velocity

of light. And as *that* is 670,000,000 miles an hour, it's not a speed that will worry us for a long time to come. At a thousandth of the speed of light one would get to Mars in a few days.

As greater speeds become available, they would not merely shorten the voyages to the nearer planets; they would also make it possible to travel to more distant worlds such as Jupiter and Saturn. Eventually, though it may take several hundred years to accomplish it, spaceships from Earth will have visited all the planets of the Sun, from scorched Mercury to eternally frozen Pluto and the unknown worlds that may lie beyond it.

What will they find—and why will they go there? The time has come to try to answer these questions—though the real reasons for going to the planets we shall never fully know until we get there. . . .

12

Worlds of Tomorrow

It has taken us a long time to realize that, in our solar system at least, there are no other planets like Earth. One of the lessons of modern astronomy is that you can forget all about the idea of walking around on another world just as you would here, breathing its air and perhaps meeting people very much like human beings. The facts are quite different—and may, in the long run, be considerably more interesting.

Ignoring distant Pluto, about which we know practically nothing, the planets fall into two sharply defined groups. First there are the four dwarfs—Earth, Venus, Mars, and Mercury—ranging in diameter from 8,000 miles for Earth down to 3,000 miles for Mercury, with Mars and Venus in between. After this there's a big jump in size when we come to the four giants—Jupiter, Saturn, Uranus, and Neptune. Jupiter is over *80,000* miles in diameter—that's ten times the diameter of Earth—and even the smallest of this group, Uranus, is over 30,000 miles through the center.

Quite apart from mere size, there's a fundamental difference between the giants and the dwarfs. For the Earth-type dwarfs are solid, while the Jupiter-type giants are not.

We're so used to our own solid Earth that it's difficult

to realize that our planet is probably a freak and is quite overshadowed by worlds ten times bigger and of a completely different composition. Jupiter (Plate 27) and its companions have enormously thick atmospheres which get denser and denser toward the center of the planet until eventually they become liquid at some unknown depth. Down in these depths great eruptions or disturbances sometimes take place, causing what one might call storms, except that they are often bigger than our entire world and may last for years. It is highly unlikely, therefore, that our spaceships will ever land on these inhospitable planets, whose atmospheres, incidentally, consist of poisonous gases such as methane, ammonia, and hydrogen. But it will still be worth going out to visit them, not only to observe them from really close quarters but because they have at least 29 moons of assorted sizes, and, on many of these, landings could undoubtedly be made.

The giant planets are all at a great distance from the Sun, and are therefore intensely cold. To them, our Sun will be little more than a brilliant star, giving practically no heat. As one traveled out toward Neptune, one would find that all the gases in the atmospheres of these planets became first liquid, then solid, because of the low temperatures. On Pluto, the thermometer would never rise above 300° below zero Fahrenheit.

One day, men will develop the engineering techniques needed to explore the frigid moons of these outer worlds. Some of those moons, such as Titan, the largest satellite of Saturn, are as big as the smallest planets, and will probably be used as bases and refueling points for ships exploring the outer fringes of the solar system. It is even possible that, some day, we may send spaceships down into the turbulent atmospheres of the giant planets them- selves—but they will be automatic survey vessels, with- out human crews.

Saturn, second largest of the outer planets, is famous for its unique system of rings, which make it one of the most beautiful objects in the sky (Plate 28). Those rings puzzled early astronomers a good deal, but we know now that they consist of myriads of particles circling the planet in independent orbits, and so closely packed that they ap- pear solid. One day, perhaps before the end of the twentieth century, our spaceships will enter those wonderful rings to discover what materials compose them. It would be safe to do this, because at any one point all the particles are traveling in the same direction and at the same speed. If a spaceship matched this speed, all the ring fragments around it would seem to be at rest, so the ship would ap- pear to be in the middle of a motionless hailstorm. The analogy may be rather close, for it has in fact been sug- gested that the particles of the ring are composed of ice.

However, let's turn our eyes inward to the warmth and light of the Sun, and see if we have better luck with our three neighboring worlds—Mercury, Venus, and Mars. We'll go to Mercury first, the nearest planet to the Sun.

Now we are at the other extreme from the outer worlds; it's a question of out of the refrigerator and into the fire! For Mercury is a little more than a third of Earth's dis- tance from the Sun, and gets seven times as much heat.

In 1889, the great Italian astronomer Giovanni Schiapa- relli announced that, after years of studying Mercury through his telescope, he had concluded that that planet never turns on its axis. As the Moon does in relation to Earth, so is Mercury fixed in relation to the Sun, Schiaparelli said. One side freezes in perpetual darkness, while the other roasts in eternal day.

Other scientists built up an image of what Mercury must be like. If you were at the center of Mercury's sunlit side, they said, the rocks around you might be at a temperature of over 700°F—hot enough to melt some metals. As you moved toward the dark side of the planet, and the Sun sank lower in the sky, the temperature would fall rapidly until there would be quite a wide belt where it was fairly temperate. Beyond this region, and covering half the planet, would be the frozen land of eternal darkness, lit only by the stars. Hanging in the sky one would often see the brilliant beacon that is our Earth, with a fainter star, the Moon, close behind it.

For 75 years, all textbooks of astronomy repeated Schiaparelli's finding that Mercury always keeps the same face turned toward the Sun. In 1965, however, Gordon Pettengill and Rolf B. Dyce, working at Cornell University's observatory in Puerto Rico, produced a stunning scientific surprise. They bounced radar waves off Mercury's surface, catching the echoes of the returning waves in a special antenna. By measuring the time between the sending of the radar signal and the return of the echo to Earth, it is possible to determine whether the body reflecting the radar waves is rotating, and, if so, how fast it turns. Pettengill and Dyce discovered that Mercury rotates on its axis approximately once very 59 days.

That swept away the old "night side" and "day side" image of Mercury. Each hemisphere in turn gets its chance to be the bright side and the dark side. There is no hemisphere of eternal day, and there is no hemisphere of eternal night. Even so, the extremes of temperature between day and night are great because the rotation is so slow; both halves of Mercury are alike, harsh, cruel places, now roasted, now frozen.

Because Mercury is a small world, its gravity is low, and a planet with a low gravity cannot keep an atmosphere, since its gases would leak away into space. Mercury must be as airless as our Moon.

Clearly, no creatures that exist on Earth could live on Mercury—but does that mean that life of any sort would be impossible there? We don't really know enough to answer that question, for life on *this* Earth is still very much of a mystery. It used to be thought, for example, that life could arise only on a planet that had oxygen in its atmosphere. We now know that this is wrong, because free oxygen does not occur in nature in any quantity. It is actually produced by living things—plants—so the first forms of life on our planet must have been able to exist in an atmosphere with practically no free oxygen.

It does seem, however, that all forms of life need water in the liquid form, and that sets definite temperature limits. If liquid water exists at all on Mercury, it would be only for the brief time in the hemispheric cycle between the periods of intense heat and the periods of intense cold. So any life-form inhabiting Mercury would need to be fantastically durable—capable of coping with the greatest extremes of climate to be found in the solar system, and capable of getting along without liquid water for perhaps 90% of the time. It seems doubtful that life can survive at all under such conditions. But we won't know until we get there—which is one of the best reasons for going.

Between Earth and Mercury lies Venus, which has often been called Earth's sister world. The only reason for this is its size, just a little less than our planet's. That seems to be as far as the resemblance goes, for in every other respect Venus is most unlike Earth.

In the first place, her atmosphere is entirely different from ours. Venus is covered by a thick, dense white blanket of clouds through which no telescope can penetrate. There are no markings at all, none of the divisions into continents and seas which would be so obvious to observers looking at Earth from space. Sometimes faint and shadowy patches can be glimpsed, but even these are uncertain and they never last for long.

As early as the seventeenth century astronomers realized that Venus is wrapped in a layer of clouds that never, or hardly ever, breaks. It was natural to assume that the clouds were composed of water vapor, like those found in our own atmosphere, and this in turn suggested that Venus was covered with great oceans and was, perhaps, a steamy, tropical sort of planet. The inhabitants of this torrid world of swamps and luxurious vegetation, it was thought, might be immense dinosaurlike reptiles, or perhaps huge insects— a population of monstrous cockroaches and dragonflies and beetles. Venus was portrayed as a hothouse planet, raw, savage, prehistoric—a veritable paradise for the big-game hunter and film producer.

Unfortunately, this exciting dream has been destroyed by the instruments of modern science. In the spectroscope which analyzes the light we receive from the heavenly bodies, astronomers have a means of determining what kinds of gases make up the atmosphere of a planet. When the spectroscope was turned on Venus, it revealed no trace of water vapor. Nor did it show any signs of oxygen. Instead, the Venusian atmosphere turned out to contain quite enormous quantities of the suffocating gas, carbon dioxide.

The lush vegetation that everyone pictured should certainly be pouring forth vast quantities of oxygen. Gradually it became apparent that the theory of Venus as a swampy jungle planet would have to be dropped. A new image appeared: that of a terrible furnace of a world, baked drier than any of our deserts by scorching heat.

The atmospheric carbon dioxide, apparently, is responsible for this broiling desolation through a process known as the "greenhouse effect." The glass walls of a greenhouse allow the heat of the sun to come in, but prevent the escape of the heat given off by the plants inside; thus the trapped heat builds up and keeps the interior of the greenhouse warm. Carbon dioxide in a planet's atmosphere functions the same way; it is transparent to the incoming heat from the sun, but blocks the escape of heat rising from the planet's surface. Warmth is retained that otherwise would have gone back into space.

On Venus, the atmosphere is perhaps ten to twenty times as thick as that of Earth, and the spectroscope shows that carbon dioxide is at least 10,000 times as abundant there. This should produce a powerful greenhouse effect that might raise the temperature of Venus as high as 800°F—making it hotter in some places than Mercury.

Space probes aimed at Venus have confirmed this grim

hypothesis. The first successful one was America's Mariner II, launched on August 27, 1962 (Plate 25). After a voyage of 109 days it passed within 21,600 miles of Venus and monitored the planet for 35 minutes at close range, sending back more data than all the astronomers of the past 400 years had been able to collect. Mariner II reported that the cloud layer was some 17 miles thick, with its base about 45 miles above Venus' surface. The temperature at the top of the clouds was −65°F; at the base of the layer it was 200°F; and on the surface of Venus it was, as predicted, 800°F. The surface was rough and dry. Mariner II did detect some atmospheric water vapor, but only about one one-thousandth as much as is found on Earth. The pressure at the bottom of the dense Venusian atmosphere was at least 20 times that of our atmosphere at sea level—a crushing weight, equal to the pressure more than a quarter of a mile down in our oceans.

The Russians launched three Venus probes in 1964 and 1965, but instrument failures kept them from transmitting data to Earth. One of them, Venera III, entered Venus' atmosphere and evidently made a crash landing—the first time man had actually reached another planet with one of his space vehicles.

Two more Venus probes went forth in 1967: the Soviet Union's Venera IV on June 12, and the United States' Mariner V two days later. The Soviet spacecraft reached Venus on October 18, releasing a capsule that parachuted to the ground. As it fell, the capsule sent information on temperature and air pressure to Earth. At ground level the temperature was 536°F, and air pressure there was 15 to 22 times that of Earth at sea level. Venera IV's gas analyzers found that 90% to 95% of the Venusian atmosphere is carbon dioxide; the rest is mostly nitrogen, although the sensing devices reported about 1% oxygen.

America's Mariner V was not intended to land on Venus. It passed within 2,500 miles of the planet, collecting information on the nature of its upper atmosphere. Generally Mariner V's findings agreed with those of Venera IV, although there were some differences, perhaps the result of taking readings in different parts of the planet. All the space probes so far have given us a picture of an alien and forbidding world, not very likely to attract tourists in the coming era of space travel. . . .

Now we'll swing outward past the Earth's orbit to little Mars (Plate 29), in many ways the most interesting of all the planets. This interest arises from the fact that it's the only planet whose surface we can see at all clearly. Mars has an atmosphere which is sometimes cloudy, but on the whole it seldom hides the features beneath.

A great deal of nonsense has been written about Mars: that it has huge "canals" and other signs of intelligent life which are visible from Earth; that it has large oceans; and so forth. Nearly all of this has proven to be sheer myth. By observing the planet patiently for many years, astronomers have built up remarkably detailed maps and have been able to learn a great deal about physical conditions on Mars. Lately this has been supplemented by data gathered at close range by unmanned space probes.

Mars is a small planet, little more than half the diameter of Earth and with about a third of our gravity. And it's all dry land; there are no seas or lakes, and water appears to be very rare. At the poles are two white caps, which shrink during the summer in their respective hemispheres and grow again during the winter. Earth, seen from space, shows similar caps: the snows of the Arctic and Antarctic regions. The fact that the Martian polar caps sometimes disappear completely during the summer proves that they must be very thin, and they may consist of layers of frost only a few inches deep. So they cannot be compared with the thick icecaps of Earth.

There's an atmosphere, but one thinner than at the top of our highest mountains. You would have to go fifteen or twenty miles up into our stratosphere before you found pressures as low as at the surface of Mars. The atmosphere is probably mostly nitrogen, and contains no oxygen that can be measured by our spectroscopes. So we must write off Mars, like all the other planets, as the abode of life of the kind we know.

Yet quite possibly there is life there. Mars has seasons just as the Earth has (though they are almost twice as long) and large areas of the planet around the equator change color in the spring and summer in the way one would expect vegetation to behave. It must be vegetation of a very primitive kind, perhaps not unlike the lichens which may be found on weathered rocks.

Because of its greater distance from the Sun, Mars is a good deal colder than the Earth. Its thin atmosphere is also a much less effective "heat blanket," and for this reason the planet's nights and winters are very cold indeed. They are not so cold, however, that suitably evolved life-forms could not hibernate through them. In Mars' temperate zones, a summer day may see temperatures of 40° or 50°F, with a sudden plunge to −100° or lower after dark.

Instrument readings show that at midday in the Martian tropics during summer the temperature sometimes reaches 87°F, and the general daytime range there is a comfortable 50° to 70°F, though night brings a drop far below the zero line.

Beyond this, there is no evidence at all for the existence of animal life, still less intelligent life, on Mars. At the beginning of the century there was much speculation about the so-called canals on the planet—markings which some astronomers considered too straight to be natural. However, though there are undoubtedly some curious lines on Mars, very few astronomers today take seriously the idea that they are artificial. Since even our biggest telescopes are incapable of seeing anything on Mars less than about 20 miles in width, they have been no help in settling the controversy over the canals.

The thin atmosphere, by exposing Mars to meteor bombardment from space, has decorated the landscape in a different way. This was somewhat surprisingly demonstrated by the voyage of Mariner IV, the first successful Mars probe. Launched by the United States in November, 1964, Mariner IV reached Mars on July 14, 1965, passing the planet as planned at a distance of about 6,000 miles. During the 25-minute fly-by, the probe took 22 pictures of the Martian surface, which were relayed to Earth. The photographs somewhat unexpectedly revealed Mars to be almost as pockmarked by craters as our Moon. Neither science fiction writers nor scientists had predicted this. Mariner IV showed that the Martian atmosphere must be even thinner than had previously been thought.

Mariner IV solved few of Mars' mysteries. Each photo

that it took covered an area of only 300 square miles, too small to tell us much about large-scale surface features, and yet the height from which the pictures were taken made impossible the detection of any individual feature more than two miles across, too large to give up a knowledge of surface details. So we found out nothing about the presence of vegetation on Mars. (One should note, though, that aerial photographs of the western deserts of America taken from a height of only 10,000 feet also failed to show plant life.) Mariner IV told us nothing about the possibility of animal life on Mars. (Again, it must be considered that 20,000 photographs taken by Tiros satellites 600 miles above the Earth show no evidence at all of life on our planet.) Nor was Mariner IV any help in the canal dispute, either; except for one barely visible trace on one photograph, its pictures showed no marking that could be considered a "canal."

Two subsequent Mars probes provided more details, but still no basic revelations. Mariner VI, launched in February, 1969, crossed the face of Mars in its equatorial region at a height of 2,000 miles on July 30. It took 74 pictures and gathered data about the Martian atmosphere, finding carbon dioxide, oxygen, and hydrogen in it, but, oddly, no nitrogen, at least in the upper layers. Mariner VII was launched late in March, 1969, and crossed the south pole of Mars on August 5, taking 91 pictures. It found snowdrifts three feet deep there, and a polar temperature of $-253°F$ (Plate 26).

Manned flights to Mars will probably be coming up in the 1980's. Until then, we will have to make do with our present picture of the planet: a desert world, bare, dry, and generally cold. A biting wind blows over a dismal rust-red landscape, stirring up blinding sandstorms. There are no lakes, streams, or rivers, not even ponds. Plant life, if it exists at all, most likely consists of tough, simple varieties clinging close to the ground. The monotony is broken only by the many craters, large and small, and by an occasional thin cloud of dust. Not a very inviting place, all in all, though by comparison with such planets as Jupiter or Venus or Mercury an Earthman would find it quite cozy and comfortable!

13

The Challenge of the Planets

Many people, when they hear what hostile conditions we shall encounter on the other planets, are inclined to ask: "Why bother about space voyages if things are so unpleasant outside the Earth?" That's a good question, and one that must be answered convincingly.

There are many reasons why explorers have endured great hardships and often given their lives to reach out-of-the-way places on this Earth. Curiosity alone isn't the only answer, though it is an important one. The men who finally conquered Mount Everest knew that they would make no wonderful discoveries when they reached the summit: the top of one mountain is much the same as that of any other. But, as long as Everest remained unclimbed, it was a challenge—a challenge that had to be met for its own sake. That most people feel this way was proved by the enormous pride and interest aroused by the triumph of the Everest expedition.

The planets represent a similar challenge. Even if there were no practical value in going to them, men would certainly undertake the long journeys as soon as it became technically possible to do so. There are a lot of places on our own planet that are not worth visiting—but people have been there just to make sure!

However, travel into space will be very much worthwhile, even though at the present time we can guess at only a few of the things that may be discovered on the other planets. There is hardly a single branch of science that will not make giant steps forward when the conquest of space begins. It is just because conditions *are* so different on the other planets that we may expect to make new discoveries there. Even if we do not encounter the weird life-forms beloved by science-fiction writers, there will still be enough to keep geologists, physicists, and chemists busy for centuries.

But what use is scientific knowledge? Well, in the first place, it is valuable for its own sake: it enables us to have a better understanding of our place in the universe, and it satisfies that curiosity which, more than anything else, distinguishes man from the animals. All the greatest scientists sought knowledge simply because they wanted to know, not because they were looking for any particular thing of practical value.

Yet, of course, scientific knowledge *is* of enormous practical value: our whole civilization, all the machines we use, the clothes we wear, the food we eat, the enter-tainment we see on TV or motion-picture screens, the medications we take when we are ill—all these things are the result of scientific discoveries. All things that increase knowledge also increase power; one must understand the universe before one can do anything about it. It is true that knowledge can be used for good or evil, but that is a moral problem, not a scientific one. The scientist is not responsible for the fact that the study of bacteria can give us both penicillin and germ warfare.

The space program has already yielded a host of technological developments of great value—from improved means of communication and weather forecasting to tremendous advances in electronic instrumentation. When we reach the planets, we will discover many strange and valuable minerals, and in time it will be worthwhile bringing them back to Earth to replace our own rapidly diminishing resources. But in the long run, our most precious import from space will be a greater understanding of the challenging universe in which we live.

To what extent the other planets will be actually colonized by people from Earth, it is quite impossible to predict. Until we have discovered a great deal about them by direct exploration, we obviously will not know which planets are worth developing and which will be left alone. There is no doubt that even in the present stage of space technology it would be possible to maintain bases on the Moon and the nearer planets: the only real problem is that of the immense cost of such projects.

Engineers and architects have already amused themselves by considering some of the problems that will have to be met when we attempt to construct the sort of lunar base mentioned in Chapter 10. The Moon, having no atmosphere at all, represents rather an extreme case, but similar difficulties would have to be overcome on planets like Mars and Venus, which have unbreathable atmospheres. (The fierce heat of Venus is another problem entirely!) Our first bases on the Moon might be constructed from flexible domes, blown up by the air pressure inside them. They would, in fact, be rather like giant balloons (Plate 30), which could easily be carried and then inflated on arrival. Entry and exit would, of course, be through airlocks. Experimental buildings of this kind have already been made, and because they do not require any supporting pillars—the internal air pressure holds up the entire weight—they could be of enormous size if necessary. Large enough, perhaps, to enclose entire cities, when the time comes to build cities on Mars or Venus.

Fantastic? Certainly not, when one thinks of all that has happened in the last hundred years, and remembers that thousands—indeed, millions—of years lie ahead of us.

One day, all the planets of the Sun will have been explored, just as all the Earth is today. Mars, Venus, Ganymede, Titan, Phobos will be names as familiar as New Zealand, Canada, Peru, South Africa—countries which were once unknown, which once took longer to reach than the planets will a hundred years from now. The frontier will move outward from Earth, past the frozen worlds at the fringes of our solar system, until at last men are looking out across the great abyss, with all the planets behind and nothing between them and the incredibly distant stars. Across that gulf light itself, the fastest thing in the universe, takes years to travel. Yet out there must lie other solar systems, some of them with planets much more like Earth than are any of the other worlds of our own Sun. And somewhere among the thousands of millions of stars scattered throughout space there must surely be other intelligent races, many of them far in advance of our own. One day we shall meet them: it may not be for thousands of years, but that is the ultimate goal of astronautics.

We may never actually meet them face to face; contact may be made by automatic spaceships that will return to Earth many generations after they have set out, bringing back the knowledge their cameras and recorders have obtained. Or perhaps medical science may discover ways of permitting the spaceship crews to "hibernate," so that they may be able to travel on journeys lasting for centuries. Or perhaps, though all the scientific evidence is against it, the speed of light may prove to be no greater obstacle than the speed of sound, so that we may achieve such velocities that men will be able to travel to the stars and return in a single lifetime.

We do not know—but we can be sure that, even if we never reach the stars, the planets of our own solar system will keep all our scientists and explorers busy for as far ahead as imagination can go.

14
The Road Ahead

In the last chapter, we looked a long way ahead and touched on scientific achievements that none of us will live to see. Yet in the near future we may expect to see more or less permanent space stations placed in orbit several thousand miles up and the first permanent bases established on the Moon. Then—within ten years or less after this book is published—we should witness the departure of manned expeditions to Mars. Unmanned space probes will be going off to more remote planets such as Jupiter and Saturn. And by the end of the twentieth century even the most distant reaches of the solar system should have felt man's impact.

The technical skills for accomplishing all these things are already within our grasp, essentially. It is no longer necessary to speculate on *whether* we will ever reach Mars or Venus. The only question is how soon we will care to do so.

The time schedule for the exploration of the solar system depends largely on financial matters. Entering space is an unbelievably expensive proposition, involving sums running into many billions of dollars. Immense as such amounts sound, they nevertheless are available, provided such powerful nations as the United States and the Soviet

Union care to make the money available. The entire cost of the United States' ten-year program to reach the Moon, after all, was somewhat less than the $25 billion that this country spent in 1970 on the war in Vietnam alone.

At the time these pages are being written, the space program in the United States is undergoing severe cutbacks. Not only has the expenditure in Vietnam been a heavy drain on the American economy, but many intelligent Americans have begun to ask whether it makes sense to send rockets to Mars when such problems as poverty and pollution remain unsolved at home. In Russia, too, there has been some slowing of the once ambitious space program, although the cutbacks there do not seem to have been as harsh in the United States.

If these attitudes prevail, the timetable for man's great space adventure will of course be vastly delayed. Only a major government, at present, can afford to explore space; and if such governments will not spend the money, no spaceships will go forth. But it seems likely that the hostility toward space endeavor in the United States is only a temporary phenomenon, brought into being by the strain of enduring the costly and disruptive Vietnam operation. As that unhappy enterprise recedes into the pages of history, the United States will surely return to the dynamic outlook that sent the Apollo spacefarers to the Moon—especially if the Soviet Union should continue to make important space accomplishments of its own. Before this book is many years old, then, we may be reading newspaper accounts of renewed space activity. We *must*, in fact—for no society has ever been able to survive for long once it has turned its back on its own frontier, and space is the only remaining frontier for twentieth century man.

There are many young people nowadays who are anxious to play a part in the further development of space travel; perhaps you are one of them yourself, and want to know the best way to set about it. You must recognize right away that there is no easy road, and that in this field, as in any other, years of hard work and study are necessary.

Astronautics now embraces so many different branches of science and technology that one could specialize in almost any subject and still contribute something to the crossing of space. Electronics, chemistry, aerodynamics, pure mathematics, astronomy, medicine, structural engineering, metallurgy, nuclear physics—all these and many more are involved in the building of spaceships. So your choice is a wide one. Study hard at scientific subjects, and follow whatever practical hobby you can (for example, astronomy with homemade telescopes, building model aircraft and radios, even tracking the radio signals of the satellites now in orbit). Then, having specialized in technical subjects at school, either take a science or engineering degree at college, or go into some industrial firm where you can get practical experience and continue spare time studies through the apprentice training programs now widely available. And, of course, read all you can about space flight*: there are many books on the subject, some of them quite advanced. Here are some examples to start with, which will lead you on to further reading:

CLARKE, ARTHUR C. *Man and Space.* New York: Time-Life, 1969.

CLARKE, ARTHUR C. *The Promise of Space.* New York: Harper & Row, 1968.

LEY, WILLY. *Rockets, Missiles, and Men in Space.* New York: The Viking Press, 1968.

SILVERBERG, ROBERT. *The World of Space.* New York: Hawthorn Books, 1969.

VON BRAUN, WERNHER, and ORDWAY, FREDERICK I. *History of Rocketry and Space Travel.* New York: Thomas Y. Crowell, 1969.

Several of these books contain paintings showing what we believe conditions are like on the planets and some of their moons. One day, if mankind's thrust into space continues to advance as it has done thus far, *you* may be able to compare those imaginative forecasts with the reality of other worlds.

* One of the best places to find straightforward accounts of space developments—with beautiful color illustrations—is *National Geographic Magazine.* And the National Aeronautics and Space Administration (Washington, D.C., 20546) publishes many leaflets, brochures, and scientific reports covering every phase of its activities, for the general public as well as for experts.

Anyone *seriously* interested in space travel should consider joining the American Institute of Astronautics and Aeronautics, 1290 Avenue of the Americas, New York, 10019, or the British Interplanetary Society, 12, Bessborough Gardens, London, S.W.1. Though most of these societies' publications are highly technical, and full membership is restricted to qualified engineers and scientists, they are glad to help students and young people.

Index

Acceleration, weight caused by, 43–44
Airplanes, 7
Alcohol as rocket fuel, 15
Aldrin, Edwin E. Jr., 51–52
Anders, William, 51
Apollo missions, 29–30, 49–52
  Apollo VIII, 51
  Apollo IX, 51
  Apollo X, 51
  Apollo XI, 51–52, 87–88
  multistage rocket used in, 29–30
Armstrong, Neil, 17, 51–52, 87–88
Army, U.S., 38
Artificial satellites, 53–59
  communications, 55–58
  first successful, 39–41
  gravity and, 36–38
  military reconnaissance, 59
  scientific data obtained from, 53–55
Astronauts
  spacesuits of, 45
  training of, 44
  See also specific names
Astronomical observation
  from artificial satellites, 54–55
  from Moon, 88
Atlas missile, 46, 49
Atmosphere
  of Earth, 7–8
    density of, 34
    discoveries about, 4
  of other planets, 77, 103
    Jupiter, 103

    Mars, 111, 112
    Venus, 107–10
Atomic energy
  rockets using, 30–32
  wartime development of, 13

Balloons, 8
Belka, 46
Belyayev, Pavel, 48
Bergerac, Cyrano de, 4
Borman, Frank, 50, 51
Braun, Wernher von, 9
  space satellite research by, 34, 38–40
  V-2 project directed by, 13, 15

Chaffee, Roger, 48
Collins, Michael, 51
Combustion chamber of rocket motor, 18
Communications Satellite Corporation (Comsat), 58
Communications satellites, 55–58
Craters
  on Mars, 112
  on Moon, 88–89
Cunningham, R. Walter, 51

Discoverer I, 40
Dyce, Rolf B., 105

Early Bird satellite, 58
Earth
  atmosphere of, 7–8
    density of, 34
    discoveries about, 4

125

Format by Kohar Alexanian
Set in 11 pt. Caledonia
Composed, printed, and bound by The Haddon Craftsmen, Inc.
HARPER & ROW, PUBLISHERS, INC.